Rhonda Maxwell's

Smart Shopping
&
Good Cooking

Illustrations - Frances Mote

Protter Publishing Corporation
Toronto

Protter Publishing Corporation
Suite 701
357 Bay Street
Toronto, Ontario
M5H 2T7
Canada

Publisher: Protter Publishing Corporation
Editor: Audrey Little
Front & Back Cover Design: Nigel Protter
Front Cover Photograph: Dimitri Mavrikis
Charts: Nigel Protter
Design, Composition & Typesetting: Nigel Protter

Canadian Cataloguing in Publication Data

Maxwell, Rhonda
Smart Shopping & Good Cooking

ISBN 0-921288-00-X

l) Marketing (Home Economics)   2) Cookery 3) Title

Printed and Bound in Canada

About the Author

Rhonda Maxwell is best known for her weekly show on Global Television "**Rhonda Maxwell-SuperShopper**" which ran for five years. She is also the author of two unique books: "**SuperShopping and You**" and "**Be A Better Grocery Shopper**". Rhonda previously wrote a consumer column on the subject of grocery shopping which appeared in several daily and weekly newspapers across the country. She is a recognized authority across Canada on the subjects of grocery shopping, couponing, refunding and sensible cooking.

*This book is dedicated to
"le petit Grenouille" with much love.*

Forward

Margaret Visser in **Much Depends Upon Dinner** said "However humble it may be, a meal has a definite plot, the intention of which is to intrigue, stimulate and satisfy."

Eating for many people is a most pleasurable activity. Shopping for food is not. "Smart Shopping & Good Cooking" is intended to make the whole process easier and more effective so that you, too, can truly enjoy your personal creations.

Acknowledgements

No book is ever solely the work of just the author. It is always the combined effort of many who contribute their time and their wisdom, offering much valued opinions in order to make the dream a reality. This book is no exception. The contributions made by some are not as obvious, even to themselves, and they, therefore, deserve to be acknowledged.

Audrey Little, my steadfast friend who helped in the many re-writes, editing and proofing, at the same time made it seem like fun, was an invaluable help. Nigel Protter taught me how to use a computer, making the dreaded task of the aforementioned re-writes seem less painful. Nigel is also responsible for the creative format, design of the entire book, its charts and cover. Bernard Protter is to be credited with cracking the whip when I suffered from short-lived bouts of lethargy. These three people donated their time and energy while being consistently patient, supportive and encouraging, for which I am truly grateful.

Frances Mote is the talented artist whose drawings are shown throughout the text. I think they are delightful and I am confident that you will enjoy each and every one of them.

I would also like to thank Recipes Only, Foodland Ontario, The Ontario Milk Marketing Board and the makers of Kahlua Coffee Liqueur for allowing me to use some of their terrific recipes.

Wayne Mouland, Vice President and Research Manager of A.C. Nielsen Company of Canada Limited, was instrumental in providing the abundance of research material for the coupon/refunding sections for which I am most grateful. George Condon, Publisher and Editor of Canadian Grocer, offered both research material and his valuable time in the early stages of the writing of this book which made launching this project possible.

I would also like to thank Mr. David Nichol of Loblaws and Mr. Alister Graham of Oshawa Food Group who were both kind enough to share their thoughts and views with me.

Mrs. No-Name has been both a dear friend and a source of culinary tales. She really is a very good cook!

And finally, my three little, long suffering dumplings, (who are not so little any more), Ijade, Ryen and Ramsey, who, with their relentless appetites, have provided grist for the mill over the years and have also maintained their sense of humour and patience through yet another drawn-out **epistle according to Mum!**

Introduction

Grocery shopping, for me at least, is a challenge not a chore. Many years ago I did a close examination of the amount of money I was spending at the supermarket every week. I decided that I was spending more than I really needed to. Having ascertained this, I set out to do something to improve my shopping skills. I devised a system I called "SuperShopping", which has worked for me over the past 10 years. Two books have been spawned in that time, each dealt with different shopping problems and solutions. Why, then, another book?

While the food industry, from decade to decade, always seems to remain the same, changes or improvements are being made constantly. Many people, from all walks of life, of all ages, start shopping and cooking for the first time. For the most part, some of us are not fully prepared for the experience.

Smart Shopping & Good Cooking is intended to help the inexperienced shopper and chef, make an easy transition to someone who can at least enjoy the process. This book is merely a guideline, providing the basic steps towards becoming a better grocery shopper. My wish is that it will help you achieve a level of expertise which should save you time and money in both the supermarket and the kitchen.

General wisdom

There are three constants in life which are inescapable and which forever need to be dealt with:

- FOOD
- SHELTER
- CLOTHING

Of the three, food is the only constant which, being consumed, must be provided for daily. Barring dramatic changes, shelter and clothing may require updating and replacing, but not nearly on the repetitive scale as is the need for nourishment.

We eat whether we are hungry or not. We eat whether we are rested or tired. We eat when we are sick or healthy. We eat when we are sad or happy, bored or stimulated, overworked or idle. We eat whether we are single, married or divorced. We eat when we are young, (moments after birth), as adolescents, middle-aged or, finally, when old. We always eat!

We eat for social reasons, business reasons, health reasons, good and bad reasons. We eat alone or together with other people. We eat sitting down, laying down and standing up. We eat while watching TV, listening to the radio and at the movies. We eat inside and outside our homes. We eat at friends, relatives, neighbours, in restaurants and hotels.

We eat when we fly, when we walk, go by train, car, truck or bus. We eat with our hands, with cutlery or with chopsticks. We eat at elegant restaurants, greasy spoons, fast food outlets or from vendors on the street. We eat at fairs, exhibitions, trade shows and farmers' markets. We eat too little, just the right amount and, quite often, too much. Everyone of us must eat, as we always have and forever will. Until such time as the "once a day" pill is invented (God Forbid!), we will continue to do so.

Since many of us must purchase our food, rather than grow it ourselves, we should accept that the grocers, of whatever description, should be our best friends. We depend on them and their suppliers to provide us with the selection and variety of foodstuffs which make life itself not merely possible, but also enjoyable.

Contents

Adam and his rib

Once upon a time there was Adam and his spare rib. Presto, Eve emerged.

They moved into a nice comfortable cave. As should be expected, they were always hungry.

Adam set out on an almost daily basis to hunt for food so as to provide for himself and his mate. As they multiplied, and did so miraculously, there were forever more mouths to feed. Therefore, the hunting and gathering process became increasingly more difficult.

Much transpired between the time of the cave dwellers, the establishment of towns and the emergence of city dwellers. In between, the barter system was developed. Food and services were traded amongst clans or groups of people.

The first capitalists

Slowly, enterprising individuals set up shops to trade and sell merchandise needed by the general public.

The history of the development of the food distribution industry in Canada and the United States is both interesting and difficult to trace. (I have mentioned the U.S. experience on the following pages as much of what happened there, as it still does today, affected the Canadian grocery industry.)

According to George Condon, Publisher and Editor of **Canadian Grocer,** the system by which food reaches our tables from its numerous sources of supply is a complicated process evolving over the past 277 years.

It would be impossible to provide a complete background on the evolution of the food industry for it requires a book of its own. Therefore, I have provided an overview of how it all came about. I hope from this you will understand some of the inner workings of your local grocer and the thousands of people who make it all possible.

On the occasion of MacLean Hunter's 100th anniversary, **Canadian Grocer** published a special issue. "I saw changes which were evolutionary, not revolutionary. Parts of the modern day supermarket as we know it today, were experienced decades ago by early shoppers,"said George Condon.

It appears that in spite of the important changes our world has experienced, our parents and grandparents, as early as the late 20's and early 30's, were offered similar types of shopping opportunities. Some of the basic elements of the food distribution industry have remained constant over the years. As trends and fads come and go, the mix merely changes according to what the retailers and manufacturers perceive to be the consumers' needs. Much of what you will read on the next few pages will sound very familiar. What may appear to be new to the current generation of shoppers, is not necessarily new to the industry.

The opening up of Canada

1670   The Hudson's Bay Company received charter.[1]

1770   Joseph and Co. sets up a grocery business on the east coast.

1774   York Factory outlet of The Hudson's Bay was augmented by Columbus House.

1770's Barter used as main form of payment in exchange for goods and services rendered.

As our country developed from the east to the west, merchants responded to the needs of the pioneers settling the land. As settlements grew in size from garrison outposts to small towns, which in turn expanded to become larger cities, the need to provide the basic food stuffs and other essential items also increased.

By the 1880's the main food supplied was flour, beef, pork, sugar, tea, spices and molasses. These goods were stored in large bulky containers behind the counter and the owner or the "provisioner" served the customer directly out of these containers.

As in so many other aspects of our lives, socio-economic and political forces also shaped the development of the food distribution industry. For instance, the dramatic change from bulk food to packaged food has been noted as the forerunner to what we now call "branded merchandise".

1839 First fish canned in the Bay of Fundy area.

1856 Borden Condensed Milk started working on plans for canning milk.

1869 Cans were still being made by hand in Grimbsy, Ont.

1870 First automatic canning line opened in Syracuse, New York.

1880 Efforts were made to expand the canning industry in Ontario.

1886 Borden successfully created its first can of condensed milk.

The coming of age

Up until the early 1900's, it seemed as though the industrial revolution had forgotten the food industry. As factories sprung up over the land, mass producing everything from cars, clothes and shoes, small outlets such as bakeries, butchers, corner stores, fruit and vegetable stands, still supplied the bulk of the food to America. Even though the beginnings of the "chains" had surfaced, they were still for the most part one-man operations.

1908	H.M. Jenkins opened first chain store in Calgary.
1919	T.P. Loblaw, in partnership with J.M. Cork, opened first self-serve in Toronto.
1920's	Shift was seen from counter serve and credit to self-serve and cash and carry.
1928	Stores began grouping "like products" together.
1930	Mike Cullen, opened first supermarket in Jamaica, Long Island, New York.

Mass merchandising

1930's Large warehouse outlets were introduced.

Cash register tapes with purchase breakdowns were introduced.

Wire services brought national brand advertising to the consumers.

Food Day advertisements appeared for the first time.

Radio became a popular means of advertising.

1940's Supermarket chains became an established fact in North America.

Shoppers used market baskets or wagons and saved their paper sacks for re-use.

New advancements in cash registers, checkouts, store refrigeration and freezing were made.

1945   Consultants offered advice on floor layouts to help increase store efficiency.

Packaging

Equally important was the discovery of cellophane. Today we know it as plastic wrap. This one product allowed for the pre-packaging of many products which further aided the self-serve concept. It was during the first formative years of the development of supermarkets that No-Frills shopping became dominant. In these stores, general goods were sold 8-15% cheaper as compared to products sold over the counter. The change from bulk packaging was the forerunner to branded products.

Change in direction

1945   Rationing of gas made one-stop shopping a must.

Consumers travelled to supermarkets to stock up.

During the war supermarkets helped families plan meals using ration cards.

Pre-packaged salt and sugar became popular.

Tea and coffee were packaged in smaller portions.

Vinegar and molasses became available in tins and glass.

1947   Biscuits were sold in tins lined with moisture-proof paper.

In 1947, Canadian Grocer asked senior executives with at least 40 years experience in the business to reflect back on their careers and comment on any changes they had noted. Frank W. Shirriff, Shirriff's Limited, is quoted as saying the most revolutionary changes in the industry were as follows:

- the change from bulk to packaged foods.

- advent of food packaged in hermetically sealed containers.

- store modernization including self-serve meat departments and improved refrigeration, the introduction of new approaches to advertising and merchandising.

He went on to say "the entire transition is a splendid example of competitive operations in a free economy under democratic laws providing the public with better service at a reduced cost to them".[2]

Post War Market Trends

1950   Television became a very powerful tool for national brand advertising.

Average supermarket carried between 2,000-3,000 items.

1960's Construction of new roads played an important role in the vital need for fast, reliable transportation of foodstuffs.

Pre-packaging of meats and poultry laid the foundation for the method by which we purchase these products to-day.

Number of items carried in an average supermarket rose to 5,900.

New developments in packaging equipment allowed dairies to package dairy products for self-serve for the first time.

The Food Index — the barometer by which we gauge inflation — was established for the first time.

Inflation stirring

By the mid-60's, larger stores became common, averaging about 30,000 square feet. It was during this decade that influences such as intense competition, which brought lower pricing, and the impact of consumer demands that governmental regulations emerged. Unit pricing, open-code dating and other information useful to the consumer started to appear on packaging.

1970 Average number of items carried by a supermarket increased to 7,800.

1973 OPEC lowered the boom on the west and raised oil prices.

Higher interest rates and the price of gas at the pump caused inflation to soar.

Due to the dependence of the food transportation system on the price of gasoline, food became correspondingly more expensive.

Added to the high cost of operating a super-market during this time period was their heavy use of fuel for air conditioning, refrigeration and freezing.

1978 Electronic scanning came to Canada.

Supermarketing

1980's Warehouse outlets appeared offering no frills and lower prices, as an alternative to regular supermarkets.

Average supermarket carried between 9,000-12,000 items, no frills carried about 1,000.

Increased couponing and refunding by the consumer.

Bulk food became the popular.

Coupon trading clubs appeared.

Generic products became another "line of goods" offered to the consumer.

Groceries were packed in plastic carry-out bags as opposed to brown paper bags.

1980's "Bag your own" grocery checkouts were introduced.

Sampling, fear of contamination and ensuing government regulations caused most supermarkets to close bulk food sections or to scale them down considerably.

1985 High interest rates began to relax.

More reasonable food prices returned.

More exotic foods from foreign lands were imported.

1987 Electronic couponing came to Canada.

Who's who!

Some of the key players in the Canadian food industry (listed in alphabetical order) are:

- A&P/Dominion

- Atlantic Wholesalers

- Canada Safeway

- Kelly Douglas

- Knob Hill Farms

- Loblaws

- Metro Richelieu

- Oshawa Foods (which includes Food City/IGA)

- Overwaitea

- Provigo

- Save-On

- Sobey's

- Steinberg's (Includes Miracle Mart in Ontario)

- Super Carnival

- Zehrs

Ten retail and wholesale operations control 80% of the business in the food industry in Canada.[3]

When generic products took Canada by storm in 1978 Loblaws Supermarkets went one step further. Under the leadership of David Nichol, Loblaws transformed generic products into a "brand" of its own. While some stores carried a modest line of plain label products, Loblaws launched their No Name brand with 300 different products. By 1986, this line was expanded to include over 1,000 items. The now famous black and yellow packaged products were the forerunners to the "President's Choice" line. Launched in 1985, this line now includes over 300 products which are advertised in the weekly flyers and in the well-known "Insider's Report".

According to David Nichol, President, Loblaws International Merchants Ltd., today's consumers are more price conscious, yet are equally concerned about quality. They "like new things and have become adventurous in their food choices".

He also feels that we are ready for more information about the content of the food we buy, i.e. calcium, fibre, salt and MSG. Consumers are also looking for more "freshly prepared" foods to augment home cooked meals.

Alister Graham, President, The Oshawa Group Limited, runs an operation divided basically into two groups. One is the wholesale division, which supplies the independent IGA stores, and the other is the Food City retail chain.

Mr. Graham feels that income plays an important role in the decision as to where to shop as much as what to buy. The more money at a shopper's disposal, the more likely we are to find that person in exclusive speciality shops. At the opposite end of the scale are the lower income households who in their search for nutritious, good food, at reasonable prices, are likely to travel greater distances.

"Newspaper advertisements play an important role in positioning a store against its competitors. They basically show price and item. If an item "on special" as a loss leader is one you need, then it becomes a good buy and might therefore spur you to travel to that store to pick up their specials together with other items also at good prices" said Mr. Graham.

"Food City underwent an image change in 1986-87 and has positioned itself as a good solid place to shop", said Mr. Graham. "Food City stores have become a medium-sized supermarket with a country-style general store atmosphere. As part of the growth of ethnic communities which Canada has experienced, many stores are gearing themselves to cater to this market. Food City is one of the chains which has responded to these new communities and their particular needs,"commented Mr. Graham.

The Oshawa Group has yet to build a superstore and is unlikely to do so. Given that the company has always been in the wholesale and retail business, Mr. Graham sees no reason to change. In their stores, they have simply put up walls between the operations of Towers/Food City/Drug City.

Will Canadians see "scan your own checkouts" as seen on an experimental basis in the United States? Mr. Graham felt that this type of operation is very cold and doubted whether it would have any significant impact in Canada.

I asked Mr. Graham what his prognosis for the year 2000 was and how it would affect his business. He replied that "Independent groups would become stronger. There would be an increase in the Mr. Grocer, IGA and Knob Hill kind of operations. More fresh products and additional services would be the order of the day. As the government continues to play a strong role in setting patterns for when and what time we shop, supermarkets will be forced to offer the best possible service at the best possible price in order to maintain their market share". He also added that I would receive ten different answers from ten different people, all from the same industry.

Boutiquing

As the 1980's passed the mid-way point, we saw a return of the large warehouse type stores under the banner of the **superstores.** Back in the 1930's, when this concept was first introduced, the store owner offered concessions to speciality shops such as butchers, bakers and fresh produce vendors. Today such operations are called boutiquing. Same concept, just operating in this decade under a different name. In addition, these superstores offer a wide selection of household goods, drugs, food, magazines, books, appliances and, soon, clothes...one stop shopping.

"As time becomes more precious, shoppers are willing to spend a little more for good quality products rather than making several stops" says Perry Caicco, Senior Manager, Corporate Development, Loblaws Supermarkets.

Bringing home the bacon

Technological changes, revolutions, the age of nuclear science, the computer, and world wars have all significantly altered our lives while shaping the history of the world. Yet with all the advancements we enjoy today, man must still satisfy one constant requirement which helps ensure the continuity of life — FOOD!

We bear the burden of this responsibility daily. Granted, the head of the house no longer forays with club in hand to secure the evening meal. The search today can be frustrating and tedious if we are not equipped to handle the task. A consumer who sets foot in any food store without the knowledge and proper tools is like a caveman entering a dark cave without his club.

Acquiring the necessary skills to be a good shopper is not difficult. In the next few chapters I will show you how to become a smart shopper.

The agony

Seven out of ten people will be honest enough to admit they hate grocery shopping. Grocery shopping is a dreaded, yet essential task for most people. I believe it is because most people are not adequately skilled to shop properly.

The total value of Canada's grocery market in 1985 was $35.6 billion. The average family of four spends roughly $5,200 per household or approximately 17 per cent of the total family income on food, whether it is eaten in their home or outside their home. Depending on your income, that can be a great deal of money.

Grocery shopping is not a trendy topic. It cannot be (nor should it be) compared to what is happening with The Stock Market, the Blue Jays or the Edmonton Oilers. It is certainly not as hot as some of television's night time soap operas.

It is something most of us do at least once every single week. It is a chore we all embark on with little or no training. Chances are that if your parents were poor shoppers or took little interest in passing their techniques on to their children, you, too, will be a poor shopper. This may not seem important to you until you remember how much money you could be wasting at the supermarket.

Grocery shopping has become an integral part of our lives. Whether we shop at Delis, speciality shops or supermarkets, we all shop. Until a method of purchasing food is invented that does not require us to make personal selections, we will be forced to go out shopping.

You have a choice in this matter. Unless you can coerce or delegate someone else to do the shopping for you, you can either do it and like it, or do it under sufferance or, worse, positively hate it. I believe that with a good attitude and the proper skills and tools, you can learn to do a better job. (I cannot, however, promise to turn you into an enthusiastic shopper!)

So given that you have to shop, let's take a look at what you can do as a consumer to make the job easier and, perhaps, less expensive and time consuming.

Acquiring the necessary skill

As stated before, the average family of four, according to Statistics Canada, spends approximately $5,200 per year on food. If you include money spent on all non-food grocery items, the figure would rise to approximately $6,000. You would, therefore, be spending a great deal of money.

People complain they simply do not have the time to shop for groceries.

For argument's sake, let's say I gave you $6,000 as a deposit on a new car. Would you do any of the following when shopping for the new car?

• Go to the showroom three days BEFORE new models arrive?

- Take along a tired and hungry child?

- Go right after work on the worst day you have experienced in months?

- Go when you are tired and hungry?

- Go when you know the showroom will be crowded?

- Go to any showroom without any idea of what kind of car you would like or can afford to buy?

The answer to all the questions would be NO, of course! Yet many, many grocery shoppers do exactly that. My advice to you: shop at a time that is most advantageous for you.

Why are most people poor shoppers?

In my opinion, it is a combination of lack of skills and a poor attitude. No one really teaches us how to shop. People are, by nature, most reluctant to perform any task, whether it be at home or at work, with which they are not completely comfortable. I have never met anyone who is terribly eager to do something for which he or she does not possess either the basic skills or, at best, rudimentary training.

Every year, more and more people frequent the supermarkets with little or no shopping training. This is one of the most important life skills — the proper selection of food — which in turn helps to ensure good health, at an affordable cost. In the United States, a growing number of teenagers are now responsible for purchasing the family's groceries. This can be a frightening thought. These children are not only responsible for spending the family income, but are also directly affecting the food intake of the rest of the family. Obviously, if the child is well-trained, little or no worry is necessary. Ask yourself, are your children properly instructed in shopping techniques?

Your food purchases and subsequent consumption have a direct affect on your current and future state of health. The baby boomers grew up with a dislike for additives and preservatives. This generation is now gradually aging but is keenly active in preserving health. Is it enough to hope that our children will learn by example, by osmosis or from each other?

Listed below are a few tips which can be passed on to youngsters interested in learning the art of grocery shopping:

- Remember to make a list, take it with you and refer to it while shopping.

- Always shop when you are rested, never on the way home from work or school.

- Always shop after you have eaten. This will prevent you from over-buying or succumbing to impulse because you are hungry.

- Shop by yourself, unless the person accompanying you will be helpful. Small children would rather be at home playing.

- Shop when you think the stores might be quiet. Some stores are now open 24 hours a day, which usually means the shelves are always freshly stocked.

- If you use coupons, take them with you and have them ready to hand in for redemption.

The benefits of organized, well-timed shopping are simple to remember:

- You will save money.

- You will shop less often.

- You will be making an investment in your good health and of those for whom you are shopping. Need I say more?

A small reminder: The less time you spend in the supermarket, the less money you will spend and the more you will save.

Ready, set, go!

Confuscius said: He who will not economize, will have to agonize. I have taken the liberty to improve that age old adage: He who will not organize will not economize and will, therefore, agonize!

Whether you shop at a large supermarket or at several different speciality shops, get organized before you go. Not too many of us can afford the luxury of buying food which we are going to end up chucking into the garbage. By taking simple measures to ensure that your shopping trip will be a well organized one, you will be able to save yourself time and money.

Ten years ago, when I devised my system of supershopping, I did it to avoid spending too much time and money in the stores. It has worked for me and I suggest that it might work for you too.

Put simply — what do you have to lose?

You can employ as many or as few of the steps you need to in order to get yourself organized.

Old mother Hubbard

Before setting out for the store, you should have a very good idea of what it is you need to buy, what you already have in the cupboards and what meals you are going to serve. Sounds simple, and it is!

Take, for example, a store manager for a large chain supermarket store. What manager would order from the warehouse without checking what is already on the shelf in good supply and what has completely sold out? He would not stay in business very long if he did not follow some basic rules of checking before ordering.

In addition, he cannot keep ordering from the warehouse every single day. You, too, should be doing the same checking. You have the advantage of being able to do it within the comfort of your home, with a smaller inventory to check.

Make a list of what you normally buy when shopping in a grocery store using the list I have supplied below.

Most of the checking can be done mentally, if you are the main food preparer in the home. You may have to get up to check your freezer or ascertain the amount of a product you rarely use, and see what else you have on hand.

Once you know what it is you have in stock, you can make educated decisions on what it is you will have to buy.

Inventory checklist

Dairy

Milk	White Sugar
Eggs	White Flour
Butter	Whole Wheat flour
Margarine	Rye Flour
Whipping Cream	Graham Flour
Table Cream	Yeast
Cheese	Icing Sugar
Yogurt	Spices
Cheese Spread	Molasses
Sour Cream	Lard
Cottage Cheese	Shortening
Cheese Slices	Cornstarch
Cream Cheese	Nuts
	Evaporated Milk
Baking	Condensed milk
Baking Powder	Raisins
Baking Soda	Unflavoured Gelatin
Brown Sugar	Chocolate Chipits

Lemon Juice
Semi-sweet   Chocolate
Squares
Unsweetened   Chocolate
Squares
Graham Wafer Crumbs
Cooking Oil
Cake Mixes
Coconut

Canned Vegetables
Corn
Beans
Kidney Beans
Peas
Chick Peas
Mushrooms
Asparagus
Carrots

Canned Fruit
Cherries
Pineapple
Apple Sauce
Cranberry Sauce
Fruit Cocktail
Peaches
Pears

Canned Juices
Tomato
Apple
Grapefruit
Pineapple

Soups
Boxed
Canned

Packaged
Chunky
Bouillon Cubes

Pasta
Rice
Noodles
Spaghetti
Lasagna

Sauces
Horseradish
Pickles
Steak Sauce
Mustard
Salad Dressings
Relish
Tomato Sauce
Mayonnaise

Frozen Goods
Juices
Ice Cream
Fruit
Vegetables
French Fries
Breakfast Meals

Baby Products
Diapers
Food
Formula
Cereal
Bath Care
Lotions/Ointments

Fresh Fruit

_____
_____
_____
_____
_____

Fresh Vegetables

_____
_____
_____
_____
_____

Syrups
Pancake
Corn
Chocolate

Spreads
Peanut Butter
Meat
Jams
Jellies

Cereals
Dry

_____
_____
_____
_____
_____

Hot

_____
_____
_____
_____

Granola Bars

Coffee
Instant
De-caffeinated
Ground

Tea
Bags
Iced

Cookies/Crackers

_____
_____
_____
_____
_____

Meats
Meat Pies
Hot Dogs
Cold Cuts
Beef
Pork
Chicken
Turkey
Sausages
Bacon
Ham
Corned Beef
Steaks

Household Products
Dish Soap
Dishwasher Detergent
Disposable Cloths
Powdered Cleanser
Furniture Polish/Oil
Window/Glass Cleaner
Liquid Cleansers
Floor Polish
Scrubber
Sponges
Air Fresheners
Rubber Gloves

Laundry Products
Powdered Soap
Liquid Soap
Bleach - Liquid
Bleach - Powdered
Softeners -
 Sheet
 Liquid
 Starch

Personal Care
Cream
Toothpaste
Toothbrushes
Hair Spray
Shampoo
Soap
Shaving Blades
Shaving Cream
Deodorant
Other

Paper Products
Tissue
Toilet Tissue
Paper Towels
Paper Serviettes

Pet Care
Canned Food
Dry Food
Litter
Treats

Miscellaneous
_____
_____
_____
_____
_____

What's for dinner

The making of menu plans harks back to the days when wealthy families retained cooks. The mistress of the house sat down each day with the cook, prior to sending her to the market, to plan the daily fare. This practice made sense then, and it makes sense now.

A modern advantage we enjoy over our fore-bearers, is that we can shop daily, every other day or weekly, whichever suits our lifestyle.

Plan your menu for whatever length of time suits you. Normally, a one week plan is ideal for families. Singles, young and mature, might wish to plan only for two days at a time in order to ensure variety and freshness.

There is a purpose for this very sensible suggestion. By planning each meal in advance, you will be able to more accurately ascertain which items you will need to buy in order to complete the making of the meal. By doing this, you can avoid forgetting to buy an essential item. This is important for a number of reasons.

If you forget the sour cream which normally costs $1.29, you might end up spending $15.00 when you re-visit the supermarket. When you go to the store, you will probably pick up the sour cream and a few little extras as well. That is going to add up if it happens each and every week. I recommend that if you do forget something, go down to the small corner store. While it may be a few pennies more than you would have paid at the supermarket, you will have saved yourself the time, the gas and the money spent on "treats!"

Counting the pennies

Grocery shopping is an integral part of money management for the household. It is no less important than any other fixed cost for which you must pay. Decide what you are likely to spend at the supermarket each week and then make a plan to stick to it no matter what.

It is impossible for me to say what you should be spending each week. So much depends on lifestyle, eating habits, likes and dislikes, the amount of money available and health requirements to name a few. An easy method of establishing a budget is to take one trip around the store buying only those things you ABSOLUTELY NEED. Then make a second trip around buying all the "extras". The first time around the store keep track on your calculator of how much you have spent. Do this for the "extras" as well. The next step is simple. The difference between the essentials and the extras will tell you how much more you may be spending than is necessary.

Best buys

In the olden days, (as my children like to remind me, much too often) supermarkets advertised their specials on Wednesdays. For avid shoppers getting the paper on that afternoon was something akin to Christmas. The paper was overflowing with full colour flyers showing an abundance of specials.

Things have changed in the past few years. Now flyers from some stores are distributed on Saturday, making the specials good from Monday to Saturday. Others still advertise Monday/Tuesday specials as a method of drawing customers to their stores during slower periods. In the past, most stores featured in-Ad coupons only once in a while. In fact, in 1984, only l billion "in-Ad coupons" was offered to consumers in Canada.[4] By the end of 1987, this form of couponing had increased by 900%, to 10 billion in-Ad coupons, according to Wayne Mouland, A.C. Nielsen. Occasionally, you will see coupons printed within the text of the flyer which bear computer generated numbers, usually in the lower right hand corner. This is, in fact, a manufacturer's coupon which is offered as a special promotion together with the participating retailer. Many stores wishing to remain competitive will accept another store's coupons. This enables you to shop at your favourite store while being able to take advantage of other stores' advertised specials.

Patterns and practices vary from province to province, but no matter where you live, seek out the food advertisements and use them to help you plan your shopping list.

Choose two stores which are in proximity to each other and your home. Never drive more than five miles, and certainly never drive out of your way. If you are legitimately driving by a store and wish to pop in for a good special, feel free to do so. But keep in mind that you are exposing yourself to potential risk. Unless you can shop with what I call "perforated blinkers" you may end up buying more than you intended.

If you choose to shop at specialty stores for your meat, fresh fruit and vegetables, breads and grains, you may not be interested in the food ads for those products. You should, however, remember that since all products are sold at reduced prices at one time or another, you will be able to pick up some of your staple items and household products at the supermarket. While it may sound simple, the money saved by buying paper towels at half price, laundry soap with $2.00 off or plastic wrap at 1/3 off, can be used towards a nice piece of veal or out-of-season strawberries. This becomes a simple trick of learning how to best spend your money to get the greatest value possible.

Once you have chosen the stores at which you wish to shop on a regular basis, stick to them. You can introduce yourself to the store manager as well as to section managers. This is a wise practice in the event you need a special cut of meat, have to return something or just wish to see a friendly face when you shop. By remaining loyal to one or two stores, you will become familiar with the store layout which will also save you time when you shop.

Although some stores like Food City and A&P are now uniform in layout, many are not. Therefore, once you have familiarized yourself with all the different sections within the store, you will be able to more easily find and select the items on your list. Re-tracing your steps can be very costly.

Lastly, you will be able to take advantage of the cycle of specials by tying it in with your overall planning.

Bargain hunting

Store B should be where you buy advertised and unadvertised specials only. You can keep an eye out for manager and in-store specials, but make sure they are genuinely good buys. Store A will be your major store — where you will do the majority of your shopping. In small towns, you may only have one store from which to choose. This does not mean you will not be an effective shopper. You will have to sharpen your skills to get the best values possible in an area where one chain has a monopoly.

Make your list according to the store layout for Store A. It is terribly important to construct a completely detailed list showing every-thing you need to buy. Many shoppers forget to make lists, sometimes make them and forget them at home, or make them, take the list to the store and then forget to look at them while shopping. The smart shopper makes the list, takes it along, and religiously refers to the list while shopping.

If you make a good list and use it in the store, you will reduce the chances of forgetting to pick up something vital. If you do not adopt this habit, you will run the risk of being forced to run back and forth to the supermarket picking up all the items you discover you have forgotten. This could be both time consuming and expensive.

Plotting your strategy

Your list should start where you intend to commence shopping. In many stores this will be with the dairy section. My primary store begins with the bakery and produce section but I commence at the opposite side of the store. If I were to start my shopping in these two sections, all of the fruit/vegetables and baked goods I usually purchase each week would end up at the bottom of the cart. Heavy items subsequently purchased might damage them. So decide where it suits you best to start shopping and make out your list accordingly.

On your list should be marked all the advertised specials you intend to buy. You may wish to indicate the brand, size and price, to prevent confusion when you are in the store.

For products you need, which are not on special, but for which you may have manufacturers' coupons, you can indicate the value of the coupon beside the item. This can eliminate the necessity for looking through all your coupons when you are in the store.

Let us say that you have a 50 cent coupon for an item which is not an advertised special. Upon arriving at the store, you discover that the store is running an unadvertised special for a comparable item. Without rummaging through your coupons, you can quickly ascertain which is the better buy.

You can spot a disorganized shopper a mile away. Usually this shopper is staring at the ceiling wondering whether to buy vanilla, ketchup or baking powder, sifting through coupons to find the right one or yelling across the aisle to another family member inquiring about the need for a specific item. This happens because the advance preparation was not done.

Further on in this book, you will read a chapter about coupons, but this is a good place to stress the importance of coupons. They are equivalent to cash and, therefore, the best method I know to remember to take them with you is to carry them with your money. They should be tucked in beside your wallet and calculator. And, of course, do not forget to take your list.

To shop or not to shop

You are almost ready to go shopping. You have made a list, chosen the stores, organized your coupons and set your budget. Your cash and calculator are ready to go. One last question remains to be answered: What time should you shop?

Remember on page 16, I mentioned a few tips on the best time and method of shopping. The best time is that which suits your lifestyle. If you like getting up early Saturday morning to be the first one in the store, that is when you should shop. We have learned that shopping right after work is not really a very good idea, nor is shopping with small children or unhelpful mates. Shopping when the store is freshly stocked will eliminate the need for rainchecks. You really have to be creative to convince your family that mashed potatoes, sweet peas, cranberry sauce and a "raincheck" for Sunday dinner is yummy! You can avoid this by choosing the best time for both your availability and a well stocked store.

David and Goliath

Supermarkets and superstores can be overwhelming places to shop. The average supermarket carries between 8,000 and 10,000 items. To the novice or untrained shopper, this can be intimidating. Often the choices in superstores can be daunting. The problem of where to start and what to buy can be overcome by doing your planning at home.

I believe retailers and manufacturers have the right to make money. If they make too much money at my expense, then it is usually my fault, not theirs. We, as consumers, have the right and duty (to ourselves) to make the best choices possible, given the tools at hand, for the least amount of money.

But the unskilled shopper might find himself or herself at the mercy of the company's marketing strategy if the shopping is done in an unprepared manner. Retailers and manufacturers often work in tandem to make the stores pleasant places in which to shop. Whether it be as a result of the lure of advertised specials, lost leaders, pleasant decor, the heavenly aroma of freshly baked bread, gentle soothing music or widely spaced uncluttered aisles, the unwary shopper may succumb to impulse purchases. These impulses will also be stimulated by tiredness, small children, hunger or lack of preparation, all of which are really the responsibility of the shopper.

Keep an eye out for "end of aisle displays". They are not necessarily the best buys in the store. A wise shopper takes a few extra moments to do some comparison shopping before deciding on a "special."

Remember to reach up or bend down while making selections. Well-known brand names are usually placed at eye level and are sometimes more expensive than other brands on the shelf. Taking time to check prices of comparable brands might just save you money.

Since you have remembered to bring along your calculator, use it. It serves three purposes:

- Keeps you on track so you do not overspend.

- Helps you do unit pricing and comparison shopping.

- Enables you to do metric/imperial conversion.

A metric calculator with a memory will serve you well. Some of us are still not quite as conversant with the metric system as we would like to be. A metric calculator will help you to decide which item is the better buy.

Perforated blinkers

You may be somewhat skeptical about whether or not an educated, wary shopper can resist all the temptations set in his or her path. I must admit that food shopping is a stimulating exercise. By shopping with what I call "perforated blinkers" you can keep an eye out for the products you need to buy, catch the unadvertised specials or in-store specials without adding to your grocery bill.

Listed below are a few common sense tips to help you in this endeavour:

- Stick to your list.

- Mark off each item as you place it in your basket.

- Avoid back-tracking. If you pass by an impulse item once, you will pass it up. If you expose yourself a second time, chances are you will stop and think about it. (Rule of thumb, if you have to think about it, you do not need it). WHEN you expose yourself to a temptation a third time, human nature says you WILL succumb.

Last, but not least, the store is in business to make money. You are in business to save money. Who comes first?

The better choice

In this world of vast selections, making the best choice is sometimes difficult. To the novice shopper the task may appear to be overwhelming. Of the four main food groups, produce, meat and bakery are three categories where you can take extra steps to get the best value possible for your food dollar. Aside from taking advantage of advertised and in-store specials, keep these suggestions in mind:

- Stores sometimes offer good discounts on brand name bacon to clear the stock before the "best before" date expires. In some cases the cost can be as much as half price or less. This is an excellent time to stock up on a usually high-priced item, especially if you have enough freezer space to acommodate the extra meat. Packaged bacon can be safely frozen and kept for up to six months if purchased prior to the expiration of the "best before" date. However, it is advised to use cured ham, bacon or frankfurters within a four week period.

- Brand name cold cuts can be purchased in the same manner but will only last for three months in the freezer. I recommend buying larger cuts of meat when they are on special. This way you will have enough "planned left-over" sandwich fillings at a lower cost. When you are buying freshly sliced cold cuts from a Deli section of a store, it is wise to remember that these kinds of cold cuts are best eaten within the first four days from the day the meat is cooked, **not** from the day on which you bought the meat.

If in doubt, ask the person who is serving you when the meat was prepared. It is also better to buy the meat by the slice rather than by the pound to avoid purchasing more than is really required.

- One of the most inexpensive ways to make ground beef, is to purchase chuck or blade steaks on special and grind the meat yourself. However, if this is not practical for you, always try to buy lean ground beef when it is on special. (Some stores offer reduced prices on ground meats a half hour before the store closes). The other cuts available can tend to have a higher fat content than may be desirable. As well, since the cheaper grinds will shrink during cooking as the fat burns off, the money you tried to save will go up in smoke.

- Turkeys, even out of season, are still excellent buys when you consider the number of servings provided by a large bird. Look in your favourite magazines for recipes offering creative suggestions using leftover turkey.

- During the summer in Canada we are blessed with a variety of fruit and vegetables to grace our tables. The winter months present a different challenge. Far too often, poor weather in other countries affects the quality and availability of our produce. Subsequently, it is either not available or very expensive. Should you encounter this situation, find other ways to meet the nutritional requirements of you and your family. If lettuce is of poor quality or too highly priced, make a coleslaw or a fruit salad instead. Iceberg lettuce will keep longer than the Romaine or Boston Bib varieties. Even though lettuce is uniformly priced, take the trouble to weigh the lettuce on the scales situated in the produce department. You will discover that some heads of lettuce are several ounces heavier than others. Since you are paying the same price, pick the heaviest head. Follow the same procedure for uniformly priced cabbage.

- Eight years ago, bananas sold for about 20 cents per pound. The average in 1987 was about 59 cents per pound. However, I have noticed several stores where bananas are on special for considerably less. This is a good time to buy green bananas in various stages of ripeness for use over a two week period. You may want to pick up over-ripe bananas priced very inexpensively on the discount cart in the produce section if you have a desire for banana bread, muffins or cake.

Choosing a properly ripened melon of any variety is still, for some, a mystery. Everyone has their own tried and true method. My suggestion is that you speak to the produce manager in your store to instruct you on how to choose a melon which has ripened to your liking.

- If you are fortunate enough to have a large freezer, take the time to check out the discount cart in the bakery section. You will find day-old bread, English muffins, buns, bagels, sweet treats and other delectable morsels which can be easily frozen. These goods are sold at half price. The moisture lost during the time the bread sits on the shelf will be replaced during the freezing process. The bakery goods, when thawed, will be just as tasty as when freshly baked.

Remember to keep a list of the food you have placed in your freezer. Far too often, we tend to forget what we have tucked away for future meals. By the time, we remember the quality has been affected by storing it for too long a period or by freezer burn. One solution is to use a "first in, first out"system. A steady turnover will ensure the best use of food, electricity and space. To find food quickly, tape the list you have made on the freezer door, adding and deleting as necessary.

- Herbs and spices are a delightful way to flavour and season food. Unfortunately, we often tend to buy more than we need or could possibly use in a lifetime. Herbs and spices should be bought in small quantities for two important reasons:

a)   to maintain optimum freshness and quality

b)   to enable you to buy a larger variety of herbs and spices at lower cost

For both the best variety and price, I recommend buying your herbs and spices at specialty bulk food shops.

Try not to be overwhelmed by all the choices presented to you. Instead, take the time to make the choice which offers you the best value and quality at the best price.

Checking it out

For some, the "checking out process" of grocery shopping is by far the worst part. First you have to wait in line; then another shopper just ahead of you hands over what seems like hundreds of coupons and then, when it is almost your turn, the cashier closes. It is tea time! Nothing is more frustrating. I believe you can alleviate some of these problems by doing the following:

1) Shop at a time when the stores are not likely to be crowded. A pay day is usually the worst day to pick.

2) Check out in the "Bag Your Own Aisles". This will speed up the process and will enable you to pack the groceries according to the way you intend to store them at home. i.e. all the packaged goods together.

3) Place all the items with UPC symbols or price stickers facing up for the cashier to read easily.

4) Circle all your dated coupons expiry dates for easy reading by the cashier. Mark undated coupons "NO DATE".

5) To aid putting the groceries away, place them on the belt in similar categories, i.e. bakery, all meat etc.

6) Scrutinize the ringing in of your groceries. Electronic scanning cash register tapes are a boon to consumers. A quick check of the tape will identify any mistakes.

7) Do not forget to hand in your coupons.

Homeward bound

As you can well imagine, it is important to head straight for home after the shopping is completed. Too often, shoppers plan their Saturday shopping trip as part of a larger foray. Included might be a trip to the butcher, the shoemaker, Johnny's hockey lesson or the dry cleaners. Usually, this ends up taking longer than imagined or planned. This possibility could mean that your groceries sit in the car for a few hours after you leave the store.

In Canada, common sense dictates that in the winter, fresh produce, will suffer from the cold while fresh dairy products and frozen meat products suffer from the summer heat.

If you have managed to bag your own or assisted the cashier in packing the groceries, putting them away should be simple. Most shoppers feel that the trip ends at the checkout — wrong — it ends when everything is safely stored away at home.

Here are a few suggestions to help you avoid wasting food: Eggs should remain in the egg carton to protect them from temperature changes and odours which occur in the refrigerator. Tomatoes and avocados should not be refrigerated. Mushrooms and strawberries should be washed and cleaned just before serving. Remove lettuce from the plastic bag or cut holes in it to allow the air to circulate. Bean sprouts last only 2 days in the vegetable keepers. Buy them in small amounts to avoid waste. Bread made without preservatives is best kept refrigerated. Singles might wish to freeze the bread and remove only as much as is needed. Milk in 4 litre bags can be frozen for later use.

Now you can sit with your feet up, the shopping is completed, successfully, for yet another week.

[1] Canadian Grocer, 100th Anniversary Issue, November, 1986 and
   Supermarkets: 50 Years of Progress, R. McAusland, FMI, 1980
[2] Canadian Grocer, Vol. 100, No. 11, Nov. 1986, Pg. 87.
[3] Supermarket Business Magazine, Vol. 42/#6, June 1987, Pg. 77.
[4] A.C. Nielsen Promotion Services, Total Coupon Distribution , January 1987.

The Old Folk's Nightcap

Coupons
(Increase your spending power)

Something for nothing

Coupons have been in existence since 1895 when C.W. Post of Battle Creek, Michigan introduced his "Grape-Nuts." He gave a one-cent certificate to his customers if they redeemed it at the grocery store against the purchase of his new health food product. In Canada, coupons were also used in a different form as early as 1928. Arnold Brothers' of Toronto offered 10 cent coupons in packages of ten. These were used to pay for home delivery, which at that time was starting to be phased out. The food industry, by then, had begun to shift from credit and home delivery to cash and carry. Some stores still offered the home delivery service, but at a cost.

Since C.W. Post's beginning of couponing in the 19th century, the industry has changed dramatically. In a survey conducted by A. C. Nielsen's Statistical Research Department in 1986, the number of marketer issued coupons was 4 billion. Since 1986 when 2.5 billion coupons were issued, coupon distribution has increased by 60%.

Why has the popularity of the coupon increased so much over the past years?

<u>Number of coupons distributed</u>

(excludes retailer sponsored in-ad coupons)

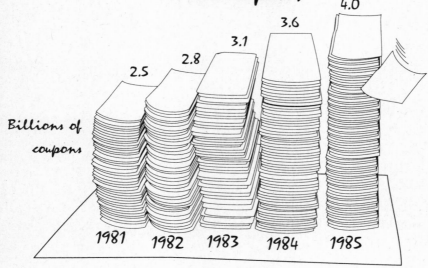

Billions of coupons

2.5   2.8   3.1   3.6   4.0

1981   1982   1983   1984   1985

Distribution figures are rounded
off to the nearest
100 million coupons

This has been a combined effort of both the consumer packaged goods marketers and retailers. The coupons were valid on brand name products, which are most commonly sold in supermarkets and drug stores.

In addition, consumers today are better informed as to their options before setting out for the supermarket or grocery store. Who can refute the obvious value of a small brightly printed piece of paper which allows you to purchase a desired item (one which you are legitimately in need of) for $1.50 less than the shelf price?

With any luck, and a bit of planning, you might even be able to secure items which have been already discounted $1.00 by the store as an advertised special, for an additional discount by using coupons.

Retailers' In-Ad Coupons are coupons you will find printed within the confines of a supermarket's weekly printed advertisement. These kinds of coupons experienced an unprecedented growth in 1986. According to A. C. Nielsen Promotion Services, "prior to 1984, in fact, retailer in-Ad (coupons) were sporadically used as a promotion tool to increase brand and store sales. In 1986, however, 60% more retailer in-Ad coupons were made available to the consumer than the 2.5 billion distributed in 1986 and 300% more than the billion distributed in 1984."[5] As previously stated, this rose to 10 billion in 1987

In my opinion this augurs well for the consumer who does not wish to spend very much time clipping, filing, sorting and retrieving coupons. This consumer does, however, acknowledge that money can be saved by the redemption of a coupon clipped from the newspaper or retailer flyer. Since many of us refer to the flyers or newspaper advertisements prior to setting out for the store, little work is required to clip the coupon and then redeem it at the store. Even avid coupon clippers who trade coupons via the mail and through clubs can benefit from flyers.

Consumers are obviously responding to Retailer In-Ad coupons as the redemption rate in 1986 has increased to 187 million of the 2.8 billion issued. In fact, in 1985, only 180 million were redeemed, compared to the 2.5 billion issued.

Consumers have also seen the value of the coupon increase from an average of 10 cents in the mid-70's to 25 cents today. Couponing is not just a fact of life within the food distribution industry but also within the drug store chains, travel industry, large department stores; all of whom use this marketing tool as an incentive to the consumer to try a product for the first time, to continue the use of the product or to switch brands or retailers.

Originally, the coupon was introduced to tempt the shopper to try a new product or it acted as a reward for having been brand loyal. Later on, competitors issued coupons to try to get the shopper to change from one brand to another. It was not until the late 1970's and early 1980's that couponing in Canada took on the same dimensions as in the United States. Couponing became big business.

A coupon is just another form of advertising, as is a television or radio commercial. There is, however, a very seldom recognized difference. The consumer benefit from a commercial is information and, perhaps, entertainment. It informs you what the product is, what it looks like, what you can do with it, how to prepare it, where to find it and sometimes how much it will cost you. The coupon can do most or all of the above plus one more important function...it puts cash into your pocket!

From the same survey mentioned on page 35, it was determined that 83% of all key grocery shoppers surveyed used coupons. Another 7% indicated that they had used coupons before, but not in the past year. Another interesting development was made evident from research that was done. Of all those surveyed, 62% had used coupons in the past month while another 11% had used coupons in the past two to three months. "These figures are also important because grocery buyers who have used coupons are more likely to be interested in new coupon offers than those who have never used coupons before. They are also more likely to notice and consider product advertising which contains a coupon".

Contributing to the trend toward a higher percentage of grocery shoppers using coupons, are the following factors:

• More manufacturers are using coupons to boost their overall sales on an ever-increasing number of products made available to consumers.

• Manufacturers are able to take advantage of a variety of distribution methods and co-operative ventures which fit into their budgets for the products they manufacture.

• Retailer in-Ad coupons made available through advertising flyers and newspaper advertisements, are offered at a higher value to encourage consumers to utilize this savings tool.

The advertising industry has become masterful in producing beautiful, attractive and interesting ads. Yet for all the work and creative effort invested in these advertisements, it is difficult to make potential customers notice the advertisement. The survey showed that consumers will notice the ad if there is a coupon within the context of the message. The advertisement by itself does nothing towards saving cash. Coupons, alone, do.

Among coupon users, 44% said they actively look for coupons in magazines and newspapers. The remainder of those surveyed said they would have used the coupon if they had noticed it.

In spite of some consumers advocating the abolition of coupons, 56% of those surveyed said they wanted to receive more coupons as compared to 15% who wanted fewer. [7]

44% of coupon users actively look for coupons:

56% of coupon users use coupons only if noticed

44% of coupon users look for coupons

Most want to receive more coupons

15% want to receive fewer coupons

56% want to receive more coupons

29% want to receive about the same number of coupons

Coupons are issued for four basic reasons;

1) To introduce a new product.

2) To reinforce a change in an existing product.

3) To increase the market share.

4) To reward the consumer for brand loyalty.

Ten years ago consumers redeemed all coupons at the supermarket. In 1986, a large percentage of all coupons redeemed was done not only at food stores and supermarkets but also in drug stores. (See chart #4). The changes which have occurred over the past few years came as a result of more drug store companies carrying or increasing their non-traditional pharmaceutical products. In addition, more companies that manufacture personal and health care products now issue coupons. 54% of all shoppers surveyed stated they regularly redeem coupons in drug stores. This is significantly higher than the figure of 24% in 1982. Gas stations have done co-operative promotions with drug stores; as have movie theatres and theme recreation parks.

Coupons come in all sorts of shapes and sizes. The coupon/refund /contest entry form has beome a popular method of couponing for manufacturers. The benefit to the consumer is that you:

• Receive the cent's off value at the cash register.

• Offer immediate proof of purchase for a refund without having to save proofs of purchase, or supply an envelope and stamp in order to receive your refund.

• Earn immediate entry into a contest for a potentially valuable prize.

How can you incorporate shopping with coupons into your regular shopping trip? Of all the shoppers surveyed, three out of five admitted to referring to the coupon file while preparing a shopping list.

The following chart shows how the share of coupons is distributed throughout Canada:

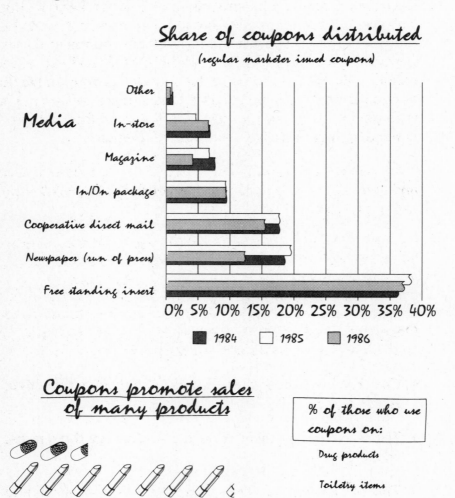

Share of coupons distributed
(regular marketer issued coupons)

Media

- Other
- In-store
- Magazine
- In/On package
- Cooperative direct mail
- Newspaper (run of press)
- Free standing insert

0% 5% 10% 15% 20% 25% 30% 35% 40%

■ 1984   □ 1985   ▨ 1986

Coupons promote sales of many products

% of those who use coupons on:

- Drug products
- Toiletry items
- Household care products
- Food products

0% 10% 20% 30% 40% 50% 60% 70% 80% 90% 100%

Coupon users=100%

Only 27% reported that they NEVER refer to their coupon file while planning a list, while another 11% said they never make a list at all.

It is equally important to remember not only to take your coupons with you to the supermarket but to redeem them as well. Of the shoppers surveyed, 91% said they took the coupon to the stores, purchased the product on the list and then FORGOT to redeem the coupon. My advice is to place the coupons or coupon file holder as close as possible to your wallet. Chances are you are not going to forget to pay for the groceries and by having the coupons close at hand, you are less likely to forget to use them.

I often advise shoppers to put the coupons, both manufacturers' and store coupons, at the front of your file. An unredeemed or expired coupon has no value to you at all.

From the manufacturer's point of view, the possibility of achieving increased sales as a result of the stimulus created by coupon advertising, whether or not redeemed, is very likely.

Admittedly there are some shoppers who refuse to use coupons. Only 10% stated that they have never used a coupon while shopping. The following reasons were cited:

• Coupons were being issued for brands of products they did not regularly use.

• The value was not high enough to encourage them to use the coupon.

• The coupon clipping and redeeming takes too much time.

• The coupons are not accepted at their regular store.

The last reason is not particularly valid as more and more food and drug stores are accepting each others' coupons. In fact, as I mentioned previously, gasoline service stations and movie theatres

Most refer to coupons when planning grocery expeditions

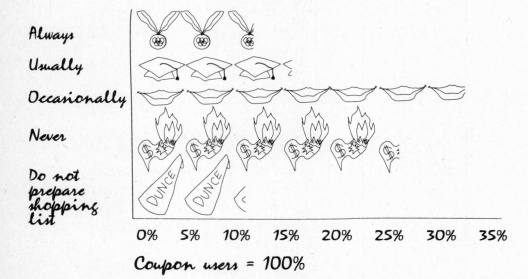

Percent who refer to coupons when preparing shopping list:

Always

Usually

Occasionally

Never

Do not prepare shopping list

0%   5%   10%   15%   20%   25%   30%   35%

Coupon users = 100%

are involved in co-op programs with chain drug stores for discounts on gasoline purchases and movie tickets.

Sometimes you may have a problem locating the product for which you have a coupon. This can happen for a number of good reasons.

- The product may not be on the regular list of items carried by that store.

- The coupon promotion may have depleted the store's regular stock. Sales may have been better than anticipated.

- The section manager may not have anticipated the speed with which the shelf stock is depleted and may not have had an opportunity to re-stock.

- The shopper may have difficulty locating the product on the shelf. Or, the section manager may have moved the product temporarily to a large display area for the promotion.

Should any of the above situations be encountered, the wise shopper will ask for help or save the coupon until the next sale.

Electronic scanning of groceries came to Canada over ten years ago. It first appeared in British Columbia and the Maritime provinces and subsequently came to Ontario and Quebec.

Electronic couponing is a natural extension of electronic scanning. The equipment already functioning at the front end (checkout) is performing a number of duties which are vital to the store's operation. By asking the scanner's computer to perform one more function, having read the shopper's purchases, enables the printer, hooked up to this equipment, to provide you with a coupon for a product you are likely to try. Catalina Coupon Systems Inc. is the first such company in Canada.

The coupons generated are a result of the computer having done an instantaneous study of your purchases. For example, if you have purchased disposable diapers, you might receive a coupon for baby food or a competitor's brand of diapers. If you buy brand name ketchup, you might get a coupon for store brand ketchup.

The benefit to the consumer is obvious. You will receive coupons for products which you are likely to try or which you buy regularly. You will not have to do as much sorting, searching and filing as you do with regular coupons. This method of marketing is called direct target marketing, as compared to the less specific targeted marketing technique of mass mailings.

You might be interested to know that soon many retailers of every description will be installing checkout scanners. That means that if you shop at a large department store, a discount store, a drug store or a hardware store you may one day see "checkout coupons". Shopper's Drug Mart and London Drugs are two chains committed to introducing scanning in their stores.

The original coupon

The good shopper knows that there is a coupon for practically every item required. In fact, coupons are available for daily essentials such as frozen juices, flour, baking products, dairy products, produce, as well as for many of our personal and health care needs. You may find cross-promotion coupons: buy a certain brand of ice cream and get a bottle of soda (to make an ice cream soda) at half price.

Maximizing your savings

If, as a Smart Shopper, you prefer to shop for only brand name products (rather than store or generic brands), be prepared to switch loyalties to a competing brand if it offers substantial savings by way of a coupon. Allegiance to one particular brand of tea, based solely on the fact that your mother always used it, may cost you a lot of money. Since it is quite possible that another brand could more than suffice, it might be worth your while to try a less expensive brand or one that is on special with the aid of a coupon.

Also, do not presume that there is a direct correlation between price and performance or taste satisfaction. The most expensive brand may not necessarily be the best. Keep in mind a golden rule of better grocery shopping - "My loyalty stops where any savings start".

According to David Nichol, President, Loblaws International Merchants - "Products like President's Choice offer better quality at a lower price than national brands". President's Choice is an up-scale store brand offered at Loblaws' stores. The product range has been on the market for just two years and now boasts over 300 items.

As you shop, make your decisions according to how much you have to spend and how much you would like to save while ensuring quality of choice.

Yet another method of increasing your savings is to buy products (on special with coupons) which contain coupons for other products you normally buy. For example, I once purchased a brand name bleach normally priced at $2.29 for a 3.6 litre bottle. It was on special for 99 cents. I bought 5 bottles for a total of $4.95 less five 50 cent coupons, bringing the total cost to $2.45. Each bottle had a 30 cent coupon for a second purchase. If I had purchased this product at full price without using coupons, the cost would have been $11.45. I saved a total of $9.00. If I used my 30 cent coupons in the same savings manner, the total cost to me would be 95 cents. Easy mathematics prove that the savings are worth the little effort required.

Listed below are the various sources for good coupons:

l)   To the Householder - Most Canadian homes receive envelopes containing coupons on a fairly regular basis. According to Wayne Mouland, Vice President and Research Manager, A.C. Nielsen Promotion Services, 6.8 billion coupons were distributed in 1986. Of these coupons 208 million were actually redeemed. In 1987 approximately 220 million coupons were redeemed against a total of 13 billion coupons issued. (The figure of 13 billion includes 10 billion in-Ad coupons issued by retailers. This is an increase of 150% more in-Ad coupons issued when compared to 1986).

2) Newspapers - There are two kinds of coupons printed in newspapers. The "in-Ad coupon" appearing in the supermarket chains' weekly advertisements is the first, and most frequently used method of couponing. For example, a store will offer a product if purchased with the coupon, at a particular price. The same product sold without using the coupon will be offered at a reduced price, lower than the regular price, but still higher than if you had used the in-Ad coupon. These coupons are usually only good for a one week period. The other kind of coupon found in the newspaper is a manufacturer's coupon and, nowadays, also a coupon for specials at fast food outlets. They usually appear on the same day as food ads and have longer expiry dates than in-Ad coupons.

3) In/On Products: Manufacturers will often print coupons on a product's packaging or announce on the outside of the package that there is a coupon inside for use on your next purchase. Sometimes it is for the same product you are buying; at other times for another product manufactured by the same company. In addition, you may find a coupon attached to the outside of the package, for use with the purchase. Both of these kinds of coupons are intended to:

- Encourage you to continue using the product you have just purchased.

- Give you the necessary incentive to try a new product by the same manufacturer.

- Introduce you to another of the manufacturer's products which you may have never tried.

- Encourage you to try a related product.

Buyer Beware.....a coupon on or in a product does not necessarily make that product cheaper. Be sure to compare the price with comparable products, including generic products, to make certain you are saving money. In addition, check if you have a coupon with a higher value for a competitor's brand which would make it a better buy, e.g. can of brand A pineapple costs 87 cents less a 25 cent coupon - net cost 62 cents. Can of brand B pineapple costs 82 cents with a 10 cent coupon on the back of the label to be redeemed on your next purchase - net 72 cents.

4) Magazines: Many Canadian magazines carry coupons in the body of the publication. The best magazines for coupons in Canada are Chatelaine, Canadian Living and Recipes Only. Clip all the coupons you can find. Trade the coupons you cannot use, or do not wish to use, with friends, fellow workers and relatives.

5) Free Hand-Outs in Supermarkets: Recently sampling of products in the supermarket has become very popular. Many manufacturers look to sampling within the store environment as a good method to get the consumer to try a new or improved product. In addition to a free sample, shoppers are normally offered a coupon off the purchase price. The store may be offering the product at a special price as well. This is a very good way to try out a new product without investing too much money.

6) Free Standing Inserts: These are the full colour glossy inserts you will find in your newspaper, usually the day the food ads appear. In 1986, 43% of all coupons were distributed through free standing inserts, according to the A.C. Nielsen Promotion Services Survey. The use of Free Standing Inserts has risen 6% since1984.

No matter where you find your coupons, treat them like money. Store them safely, remember to take them to the store when you go shopping and, last but not least, remember to redeem them!

Filing your coupons

There is a definite difference between the haphazard coupon user and the serious one who uses coupons effectively. Remember — a lost or forgotten coupon, or an expired coupon, is of no use to anyone. Organization is the key to a shopper's regular and efficient use of coupons. This is not difficult to accomplish. Since you have already organized your menu and shopping routines, the efficient filing of coupons will be a natural next step.

Coupons tucked in an envelope or stuck in a bulletin board can be lost or forgotten. Establish one place to store these valuable coupons so that they will be accessible when you need them. Some people use large envelopes kept in a kitchen drawer, others use shoe boxes, cookie tins or a recipe card box. (I found a small box, used recipe cards to make a file index and filed my coupons). It is small enough to carry around and tuck away when not in use.

Your filing system will depend upon the size of your family and on the number of products you are likely to buy with coupons. Some of the categories I have used and found suitable are:

Baby products
Baking goods
Bread and rolls
Canned fruit and vegetables
Canned juices
Cereal
Chocolate milk powder/syrups
Crackers/cookies
Dairy products
Fish - canned/frozen
Household cleaners
Jams and jellies
Laundry products

Meat
Miscellaneous items
Paper products
Pasta
Personal care items
Pet food/litter
Pickles/relishes
Potatoes/rice
Snacks/candies, mints etc.
Soda pop
Soup
Spreads
Tea/coffee
Wraps/sandwich and freezer bags

The above list is not intended to suit everyone and although it has met my needs over the past few years, you may choose to alter it to accommodate your family's needs. Some of my headings include several categories, such as PASTA: which includes tomato paste, tomato sauce and tomatoes. Under the heading of frozen foods, there are a dozen different coupons filed, but since I have used the system for quite awhile, I know just where to look for the coupons I want. Organization and familiarity are the basis of a good system — the user can then instantly locate the coupon required.

Tips to remember when sorting and filing coupons:

• highlight the expiry dates.

• sort according to category.

• file in the designated spot.

Always place rainchecks at the back of the file. However, you should try to avoid asking for rainchecks as they can throw your menu planning out of kilter. If, for example, you should want to take advantage of a special on meat which is included in your menu plan, try calling the butcher at the store where you shop, the day before,

There is a better way to file your coupons.

to make sure that the quantity you need will be available when you do your shopping.

If a special you need is out of stock, rather than accepting a raincheck for the item, ask the manager if he would consider substituting an equivalent product. (If possible, suggest one to him for which you have a coupon).

Remember, too, that you must ask for a raincheck at the time of the special or you will miss out on the savings. The raincheck usually indicates what item is on special, the size or number requested, the expiry date and must always be signed by an authorized staff member of the store. The expiry date should be heeded. If, by chance, you are not able to redeem the raincheck on your next shopping trip because the item has not been re-stocked, have it updated before it expires so that you will be able to redeem it when the item is available. Ask if the store will extend the expiration date until you plan to shop again. If you cannot use the raincheck before it expires, ask for a substitute. Rainchecks are usually issued at the service counter. Some stores do, however, issue them in the appropriate section, i.e. meat, produce, bakery.

Remember to highlight the expiry dates on your coupons as you receive them to make their handling easier. This also makes is faster for the cashier to check the dates as you redeem them at the checkout. Toward the end of the year, you should go through your coupon file and check for coupons that expire on the 31st of December. Quite a few coupons do. If you think you may not be able to use them before they expire, trade them. Coupons are now being issued with longer expiry dates or no dates at all.

Double redemption

According to Tom Mendrum, of the U.S. based Catalina Marketing, double redemption is still going strong in the United States. With over 14,000 stores in the States, competition is fierce. As a result, if one store decides to offer double and triple couponing, other stores in the area have to follow suit in order to stay in business. Couponing in the United States is very big business. Mr. Mendrum told me that while the stores will double and triple the value of manufacturer's coupons, they will not do so with store coupons.

This marketing technique is quite simple to understand and can be very lucrative for the shopper who avidly uses coupons.

Say you do your regular shopping and you have $12.00 in coupons to submit against a total bill of $125.00. At a double couponing store you will receive $24.00 off the final bill; a triple couponing promotion will net you $36.00 off. That is a substantial saving in anyone's eyes. In the U.S. many of the refund offers are dispensed by way of "coupons" for half price (one free or in actual dollar value, i.e. $2.00 off). It does not require too much imagination to discover what the final bill would be if you had a combination of regular coupons (cent's off) free offers and half price coupons. For example, a shopper might have a coupon for a free quart of milk, or a free chicken weighing not more than 4 pounds. The "value" of all these products is deducted from the bill, after being doubled or tripled. In fact there have been documented cases of shoppers being paid to take groceries away.

This happens when the total amount of the coupons offered for redemption exceeds the total of the bill after they have been tripled. So, if the shopper has four coupons or vouchers for different products worth a total of $10.00 which are FREE to the shopper, the triple value deducted from the bill is $30.00.

Since many cases of fantastic savings have occurred as a result of the shopper saving the coupons over a long period of time, you must appreciate the fact that they cannot achieve these huge savings every shopping trip.

Double redemption has made a brief and spotty appearance in Canada, mostly in Safeway stores. The fad has never really taken hold here. In the past, I have questioned this marketing tool. I do not believe that it is in the best interests of the parties concerned.

The cost of running a promotion must be borne by someone .....I wonder who it will be?

Redeeming values

Getting cash back in your hand can be a very rewarding experience. I have handed in coupons valued at as much as $22.00 for redemption at one time. Since all the coupons were highlighted (those with dates) and well organized, they took no time at all to be processed. The new scanning equipment which you find in your supermarkets has the capability of scanning coupons automatically. Soon, many manufacturers will be putting UPC codes right on the coupon. Personally, I think the idea is a good one. Firstly, the cashier will no longer have to labouriously check expiry dates. The scanner will be able to check whether or not the product was actually purchased (i.e. if you bought Monarch Flour and tried to redeem a Robin Hood flour coupon, the scanner will show "no purchase"). Secondly, the tallying of all coupons redeemed will be done at the store level by the computer rather than at a clearing-house. With all of the advantages that scanner redemption can offer us, the cost of coupon redemption and handling should be reduced. This could, in turn, create the possibility of manufacturers increasing the level and value of couponing.

Misredemption and theft

Misredemption of coupons takes place at two levels. The first is the consumer who knowingly hands over a coupon for redemption without having purchased the specified product. While this can be a serious problem, an even greater one exists with fraudulent activity.

Incidents have occurred in both Canada and the United States whereby coupons were fraudulently printed and presented for redemption. In 1987, eight Quebec businessmen were charged as part of an organization to counterfeit and redeem coupons. It is estimated that they made over $7 million before they were caught.

In the U.S. the Donnelly Marketing Corporation and the U.S. Post Office ran a newspaper coupon for a fictitious brand of shampoo called Attract. The brand did not even exist. Coupon redemption was equal to the national average for newspaper coupons. Misrepresentation at the consumer level is reported to be at about 20%. Hopefully, this percentage will not increase to a level which makes couponing too expensive for the manufacturers to support. If that happens, the honest couponers will be the losers.

Turning Pennies into Dollars

1) Have a serious look at all the manufacturers' coupons available.

2) Start clipping coupons, both useable and unwanted. Trade the ones you cannot use.

3) File your coupons for easy accessibility.

4) Regularly go through your coupon file for expired or unwanted coupons.

5) Join a coupon exchange to trade coupons you do not want.

6) Use your coupons effectively, employing as many advantages to save money as possible.

Coupons can and do play an important role in the reduction of grocery costs for many Canadians. If you have never used a coupon because you were embarrassed to do so, or felt it was not worth your while, think again. In 1988, you will be able to save as little as $200 in Canada by using manufacturers' and store coupons. Not exactly small change, in my books!

Cash for kids

In 1980, a unique and worthwhile fund raising campaign was launched by the Ontario Food Industry. Its goal was to raise money for the Variety Club projects for disabled children throughout the province. To date about $3 million dollars has been raised. By the end of 1988, 63 Sunshine coaches will have been purchased with the money raised through the Cash for Kids campaign. Furthermore, some of the money is allocated to Perinatal units in six regional hospitals in Sudbury, Toronto, Hamilton, Kingston, London and Ottawa.

In Ontario, the **Cash for Kids** campaign is a joint effort between food manufacturers, retailers and brokers. On the first Wednesday of each February, 1.8 million **Cash for Kids** coupon booklets are distributed through 46 newspapers throughout the province. In 1988, the booklets will contain 60 coupons from 45 leading manufacturers.

Since its inception, the program has been initiated by various food industries in other North American cities. For each coupon redeemed, 15 cents is donated to The Variety Club. Mr. Jack Sturman of Jack Sturman Communications Associates responsible for the public affairs for the Ontario campaign told me "if each consumer redeemed just one more coupon during the 1988 campaign, an additional $270,000 would be raised."

Sunshine coaches provided by the Variety Club organization, transport disabled children to school, therapy sessions and social outings. Without these special coaches, this would be impossible for many youngsters.

A similar campaign in Winnipeg was launched in 1982. To date, approximately $503,000 has been raised. The money has been used to provide support to such projects as The Rehabilitation Centre for Children, Variety Club's Children's Heart Centre, the St. Boniface Special Care Unit and for the purchase of a SunShine Coach. Unlike the Ontario campaign which inserts the "Cash for Kids booklet" in major newspapers across the province, the Manitoba campaign sends its coupon booklets through the mail. In 1988, approximately 270,000 homes in Winnipeg and selected areas throughout the province will receive the coupons.

The British Columbia campaign has raised $1,400,000 since its launch in 1983. The coupon booklets are distributed to all home subscribers of The Vancouver Sun/Province. In 1988,132 coupons from over 80 manufacturers were distributed. The funds which are raised are allocated to such projects as the purchase of Sunshine Coaches, the Electro-limb program and the Children's Hospital in British Columbia.

I have always advocated the use of coupons as an excellent savings tool for the consumer. By getting involved with this campaign, not only will you be saving money on products you normally buy, but you can also help to provide much needed transportation for children in your community. Since all the money stays in the province where it is raised, residents should all support this worthy cause.

Redeem your **Cash for Kids** coupons today.

For further information contact **Cash for Kids**, 416-961-7300 in Ontario. In Manitoba call 1-204-284-3911 and in British Columbia call 1-604-669-2313.

[5] A.C. Nielsen Promotion Services, Special Release, January,1987.
[6] Coupon Use by Grocery Shoppers, A.C. Nielsen Promotion Services, 1986, Pg. 4.
[7] Coupon Use by Grocery Shoppers, A.C. Nielsen Promotion Services, 1986, Pg. 5.

Refunding — A guideline

In many ways refunding, when used as a tool to increase awareness of a product, is similar to couponing. Yet this equally valuable marketing tool has additional important characteristics.

A refund to a consumer is a reward for having purchased a manufacturer's product. Until recently, consumers were required to send in a proof of purchase in order to receive their refund. This form of refunding is still the most commonly used. However, new coupon/refunds have recently emerged.

Here is how it works. You will receive a coupon-style coupon in the mail or as found in a Free Standing Insert. There is a blank space to fill in. When you redeem the coupon at the store, it is automatically considered to be a request for a refund offer when it reaches the clearinghouse. Without having to save any proofs of purchase or invest in a stamp and an envelope, you will receive your refund in the mail.

In a survey conducted by Nielsen Survey of Key Grocery Shoppers, in 1986, they found that "all these key decision making consumers are refund participants". The survey also found that 52% of the key shoppers had participated in refund offers in the past, and 35% stated that they had taken advantage of a refund offer in the past year. In actual numbers, this represents 3.2 million households who used a refund offer in the preceding year.

3.2 Million key grocery shoppers participate in refunds

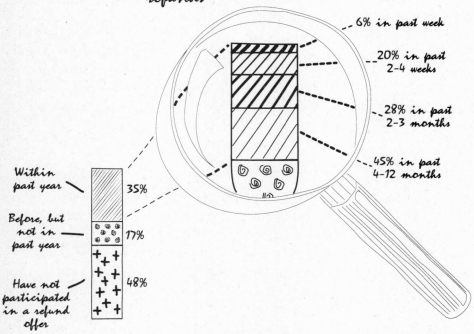

6% in past week

20% in past 2-4 weeks

28% in past 2-3 months

45% in past 4-12 months

Within past year — 35%

Before, but not in past year — 17%

Have not participated in a refund offer — 48%

Percent of grocery shoppers who submitted a refund request

An assumption can be made about the brand loyalty of refund users when you look at the low percentage of those who responded to more than two refunds in one year. The survey showed that only 15% responded to more than two refund offers and, of this group, they took advantage of four or more.

When the survey looked to see if there was a correlation between the amount of money spent at the supermarket and those who refund, it found that 57% of the households spent from $100 to $125 on groceries each week. Of the 38% of the respondents to the survey who were married, 56% used refunds.[8]

Many of us who become involved in refunding, make many false starts. When we first see the refund offer form, we have full intentions of completing the form and sending it off in the mail. Somewhere along the way we fall off the track. We throw away the package without removing the UPC, lose the proof of purchase or forget about it until after the expiry date has passed.

In any event, the refund offer is never submitted and the manufacturer has suffered what is called **slippage**. This term refers to the number of refund offers which are started but never completed. In order for the consumer to maintain interest and to actually complete the form, a reasonable level of demand must be placed on the consumer. Unless the reward to carry through on a very demanding offer is lucrative enough, the consumer will give up. For example, if you are required to purchase products within the product line of one manufacturer, which you normally never use, you might abstain. Some trade UPC's for products they do not use, for ones they need for a refund.

Taken from a Marketer's Guide to Consumer Refunds by A.C. Nielsen, are the following factors which directly influence your response as a consumer to a refund:

55% participate in at least two refund offers a year

Percent of refund participants who during the past year, participated in:

 30% – two refund offers

 15% – four or more refund offers

 10% – three refund offers

40% – one refund offer

- Type or product and the number of purchases required.

- The period for which the refund is valid.

- The value of the refund.

- The method of distribution.

Usually leading brands will experience the heaviest response to the refund offer. This is because consumers are already users of the product and do not have to go out of their way to acquire the necessary proofs of purchase. In addition to this, the length of time that consumers have to purchase the product and subsequently use the item has a significant bearing on response.

If, for example, the product is not one which the average person or household consumes quickly, it may be more difficult to respond to the refund offer in time. If it has been established that the first two factors have been handled adequately, the value of the refund is important. If the consumer does not feel satisfied that his or her efforts will be rewarded amply enough, no attempt will be made to respond.

Lastly, the response to any refund offer can be affected by the sheer number of forms distributed and the method used. Consumers can only respond if they have access to the refund request form.

While some refund offers give the consumer the option to create the UPC code by hand, eliminating the need for actual purchases, it is a rare occasion when the request form in its original form is not required.

People to whom I have spoken over the years have expressed skepticism about the value and bother that refund offers present. For some, the nuisance of gathering together UPC's from product packaging, saving them over a period of time and then bundling

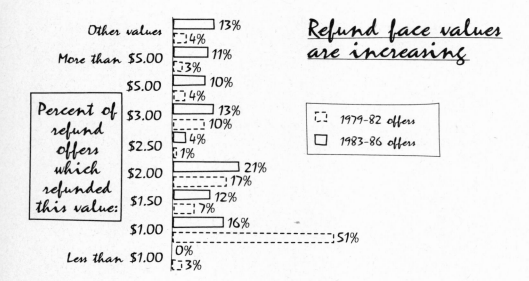

Refund face values are increasing

Percent of refund offers which refunded this value:

Value	1979-82 offers	1983-86 offers
Other values	4%	13%
More than $5.00	3%	11%
$5.00	4%	10%
$3.00	10%	13%
$2.50	1%	4%
$2.00	17%	21%
$1.50	7%	12%
$1.00	51%	16%
Less than $1.00	3%	0%

Legend:
- 1979-82 offers
- 1983-86 offers

them up to mail away is not worth the effort. When you add the cost of a stamp and the envelope to all of the above, then a dollar refund is truly not a bargain.

In the 1979-82 period, more than half of all refund offers were for $1.00 or less.[9] According to the study, only 16% of all refunds are $1.00 while the majority are at least $2.00. In addition, we are now seeing multiple refund offers which provide a 20% discount off the total purchase price.

Other trends have changed the method of advertising refund offers in the past five years. In the 1979-82 period the most frequently used method was in the newspaper mid-week food section. This has changed to in-store promotions, in/on package and "ad-pads" found attached to store shelves. In the first period mentioned, 32% of all refund advertising was done in newspapers as compared to 16% since 1983. As well, a total of 63% of all refund advertising is placed on "in/on packs " and "ad-pads " at the store level.

One of the purposes of a refund offer is to encourage a trial of the product. This is not as immediate as a coupon since the delay factor for purchasing, saving and submitting the refund is sometimes several weeks. Therefore, in order to persuade the consumer to try a product never before purchased, a refund offer is sometimes combined with a coupon to give the consumer instant savings at the checkout. Sweepstake contests are also used as an added incentive to get involved.

As a consumer, your options are quite clear....

• You can get involved in a limited way with refunding

OR

• You can get heavily involved in refunding

OR

• You can just ignore the whole thing altogether!

Some people, will not hesitate to fill in a coupon refund form, submit it against the required purchase and wait for the refund to come. If the refund or rebate is for $5.00 for purchasing toys at Christmas, you may take the time to send in the refund offer. But, you will hardly ever faithfully save all the required UPC's and send them away on a regular basis. There are those who do and they are quite successful at playing the game.

For the shoppers who are heavily involved in refunding or for those who would like to be, here is some information to help you get started.

Where to find refund forms

The necessary forms for claim refunds are available to the consumer in the following ways:

l)   In the Supermarkets: Quite often you will see a small tear-off pad of forms hanging from a shelf beside the product. These are called **store forms** and are placed in the supermarket for the convenience of consumers who would like to take advantage of current refund offers. Should you find all the forms have been used, an address where you can obtain a form is usually printed on the back of the pad. In some cases, refund forms are not absolutely required. In this event, the address to which you can send a refund request without a completed form is also shown on the pad's cardboard backing.

2) In Newspapers and Magazines: As with your search for cent's off coupons, both newspapers and magazines are excellent sources of finding refund offer forms. In both cases, you will find two different kinds of printed forms:

   a) A notice of a refund offer being made available and the address to which you should send your proofs of purchase without the need for a refund form;

   b) The actual form printed beside the notice of the refund offer.

3) In/On Products: A very common method of distributing refund offer forms is to include them in the packaging of a product. Another method is the use of the **hang tag** on bottled items, which are, however, prone to theft and removal through handling.

4) Mailings to the Householder: Along with discount coupons and offers on premium items, refund offer forms are enclosed in envelopes mailed on a regular basis to most homes. Often these forms are attached to the coupons for a particular product.

If you cannot locate a refund form for an offer you know is currently available, you should be aware that occasionally companies will honour a request if you have enclosed all the other necessary pieces of information or if you have obtained a photocopy of the form. However, there are still two options open to you.

l) Write directly to the company which made the offer: Most companies are pleased that you are planning to respond to their offer and will gladly forward the form to you. Remember to include all relevant information when you request a form in such a manner so that they can send you the correct form. Send your letter of inquiry to the customer relations department and indicate on the outside of the envelope the refund offer in which you are interested.

2) Join a form exchange or subscribe to a newsletter: You will then be able to trade unwanted refund offer forms for the ones you need. Through a refund newsletter you can advertise for forms required. Again, you will end up trading them for forms you do not need. I found the following list in The Canadian Shopper which may be of interest to you. See page 82-83 for a list of abbreviations shown within the text of the information provided about Form Exchanges.

Form exchanges

B & V Form Exchange 73 McCaul Crescent, Regina, Saskatchewan, S4R 3X3.

Trade forms 1-4-1, maximum 10, send 50 cents h/f & LSASE per transaction.

D & L Form Exchange, Box 757, Maidstone, Saskatchewan, SOM 1MO.

Trade forms 1-4-1, max. 10. Send 50 cent h/f LSASE per transaction.

Peacock Form Exchange, Box 15, Peterson Site, R.R. #3, Quesnel, B.C. V2J 3H7.

Send 10 unwanted forms for 15 preferred. $1.00 h/f , 2 loose 34 cents stamps, LSASE, $3.00 membership fee, 60 day expiry date. Receive bonus coupons, or contest forms.

Form Exchange. Marion Paquette, General Delivery, Smithville, Ont. L0R 2A0.

Trading refund forms 1-4-1. 60 day expiry. LSASE. Sufficient postage + 10 cent fee toward ad costs.

Forms Forms Forms. 337 Nelson St., Sarnia, Ont. N7T 5J6.

I will trade forms 1-4-1. I have many from which to choose. Maybe I have the one you've been looking for. Try me. I will also trade $10 c/o's for $9.50 c/o's. Send SASE and 30 cents plus 1 new 34 cent stamp. Prompt reply.

L.A. Form Exchange. #209-1304 23 Avenue North, Lethbridge, Atla.

T1H 4T6.

Send $1.00, or 3 - 34 cent stamps or $20.00 in NED coupons — receive 15 refund forms. LSASE (sufficient postage)

Mary's Form Club. Mary Read, 61 Apache Cres., Leduc, Atla. T9E 1P7.

Receive 10 refund forms for $10 c/o's and/or send 2 forms for 1 (Refund for Refund, contest for contest, etc.). Receive $10 misc. c/o's for 15 refund forms. All c/o's forms sent must have at least 60 days until expiry. Send LSASE and handling fee of one new first class stamp/each $10 c/o's sent or requested.

1-4-1 Form Exchange. Lorraine Beeching, Box 2333, Tisdale, Sask. S0E 1T0.

Send maximum 15 refund forms for exchange plus preference list. Will send 1 bonus form for each form submitted from list or I will keep your list on file and send the forms as soon as possible. State preference. Will also exchange contest and cash plus forms. Will exchange c/o's for 80% return. SASE, h/f — 50 cents.

Rainbow's Reward. #13, 654 N. Fraser Drive, Quesnel, B.C. V2J 1Z6.

Please send 10 unwanted forms + $1.00 h/f + 2 loose stamps + SASE. Receive your "Rainbow Reward" — 15 good forms plus bonus contest & c/o's. Rainbow's Reward.

Refunder Newsletter: 80 Zina St., Orangeville, Ont. L9W 1E6.

Packed with Canadian refund and contest information; form exchange service included for subscribers; $2 sample or $9 for 6 issues.

Speed Plus Form Exchange. Claudette Corrigan, 44 St. Judes, Laval, Quebec, H7W 4G6.

Forms traded 1-4-1, maximum 10 (60 day expiry date). Coupons 90% return, maximum $20.00. Send LSASE and 25 cents h/f .

Collecting qualifiers

Having acquired the necessary refund form, you will need to collect "qualifiers" to be eligible for the refund. There are basically two kinds of qualifiers. Some package designs have a special "proof of purchase" wording that proves you have purchased the product.

Beyond this type of qualifier, there is a more general list which is used interchangeably by all manufacturers. You must be aware that manufacturers can and do change their qualifier requirements from time to time. The most common qualifiers are these:

- ingredient panels

- box tops and bottoms

- tear strips

- code numbers

- neck bands from bottles

- inner liners from bottle caps; purity seals from jars

- Universal Product Codes (UPC)

The Universal Product Code (UPC) is a product identification which, when passed over a scanner, identifies the product, the brand, the size and its size.

To differentiate between "proofs of purchase" and qualifiers, refunds refer to the product packaging portions generally as "**Qualifiers**" and "**Proofs of Purchase**" only if those words appear on the packaging.

Since qualifier requirements may change, the only way to ensure that you have the right portion of the package to qualify for all the refund offers that come your way is to save everything.

Below is a list of the packaging you should save from your brand name products in the hope of sending them off for cash in the future:

Bottles:
Neck bands, cap liners and inner seals, as well as front and back labels.

Boxes:
Tops and bottoms, net weights, UPC labels, tear strips, ingredient panels, flavour seals and proofs of purchase.

Bread Wrappers:
Sometimes called for in related products refund offers. Save entire printed wrapper.

Cans:
Save the entire label by cutting and stripping or by soaking in hot water.

Cash Register Tapes:
Occasionally manufacturers will also require you to send in your cash register tape with the price of the item circled. The tape varifies that you actual made the purchase. Note: it may not be necessary to send in the whole tape. The UPC price system

should be of great help to you as the tape is so explicit you can clearly indicate the item.

Cans with no paper labels:
Note the code number of the can on a 3" x 5" recipe card and file in a special location at the back of your refund qualifier file.

Cellophane Wrappers:
e.g. cheese ... save entire wrapper.

Flour:
Save outer package and fold it flat.

Jars: (baby food etc.)
Save whole jar label by soaking it off.

Meats:
Save entire wrapper and tags from fresh meats (e.g. turkeys). Wash before storing.

Orange Juice Cans:
Save the white tear strips which identify the brand of juice.

Plastic Containers:
Save the UPC portion from the lid. Write on the back identifying information.

Plastic Bags:
Save top of bag. e.g. garbage bags.

How will you then manage to file all the qualifiers from the products you use and still not look as if you are running a re-cycling depot? Easy — break down all the packages and fold labels into the smallest possible size and then file neatly and in an organized fashion. (Just as you have done with your coupons).

The following are a few examples of how you can accomplish this with a minimum of effort.

Boxes:

(Laundry products, rice, baby food, cereal, sandwich and freezer bags etc). Remove any inner packaging. (Usually there are no identifying marks on these). Slice the box with a razor or very sharp knife so that you can fold it flat and secure with a rubber band, leave some portion of the packaging showing so you can easily identify the product. Flatten smaller boxes into manageable sizes.

Bottles and cans:

Soak off labels and neck bands from bottles. Store label and neck band together. Strip off the entire label from cans by simply slipping the end of a sharp knife under the edge of the label and slicing upwards. Cans without labels should have their code numbers noted along with any other information you feel is relevant and which you may need.

Bottle caps should be discarded once the inner seals are removed. Purity seals like the ones you find in coffee and peanut butter should be saved. Write identifying information on the back. Store with the rest of the qualifiers relating to the product.

I save all the labels, box tops, etc. in a plastic bag stored under my kitchen sink and when the mood strikes me, I sit down and file the qualifiers so that they are at my finger-tips when I need them. A few words of wisdom: Do not let it get to the overflow stage so that the task ahead of you seems to be monumental. Keep up with it as you keep on top of your coupons and you will find the task much easier to accomplish.

Filing qualifiers

You must develop a filing system that allows you to lay your hands on the qualifiers or proofs of purchase when they are needed without turning your whole house inside out and getting yourself into a frenzy. The key to the filing system is that it should be workable to suit your needs and help you find the all important qualifiers at the drop of a hat. It need not be a sophisticated system. You will need a container. An old shoe box, an accordion file, a hat box or a corrugated storage box will do nicely. This container should be small enough so that you can tuck it away when not in use.

There are two methods of filing the flattened down qualifiers. One is to file them according to category, e.g. canned products, and then alphabetically by brand within the category. For example:

Del Monte
Dole
Green Giant
Hunt's

The other way is to simply file all the qualifiers alphabetically by brand name. The following chart is a short list of some of the major brand names available in Canada.

Aunt Jemina
Borden
Bravo   Monarch
Butterball   Ocean Spray
Bye the Sea   Planter's
Campbell Soup Co.   Purity
Catelli   Robin Hood
Del Monte   Shopsy
Dole   Skippy
H.J. Heinz   Stokely's
Hunts   Tide
Kraft   Uncle Ben's
Lipton   Underwood's
Mazzola   Welch's
Miracle Baste

Depending on how active a refunder you intend to be, it's most unlikely that all the qualifiers you will amass will fit into one box. Therefore, you should have at least four or five boxes available as you acquire more qualifiers. These boxes can be labelled on the outside showing the contents. For example, you might choose to file your frozen food qualifiers together in one box and all your baking product qualifiers along with cake and cookie mixes in another. Some refunders like to place all the qualifiers from one product, e.g. cereal, into an empty but unflattened box of the same kind of cereal. However, this practice tends to take up a lot of space.

Now that you have the qualifiers filed you must concern yourself with refund forms. Since many refund offers require that you send in an accompanying form you should file these forms in a safe place. A simple method is to file them in large business envelopes alphabetically, according to product with the expiry date circled. Another method is to file them in chronological order according to expiry date and remember to check the dates periodically so you do not miss out on a refund. Pull the forms as the expiry dates approach and clip them to any qualifiers you have gathered. Then place them in envelopes with the expiry dates written on the front so that you can acquire whatever additional qualifiers you need before the due date. In this way you do not uproot your house in a frantic effort to meet the refund deadline. The envelopes can be stored in a kitchen drawer until you are ready to send them out.

Collecting the money

Having gathered together the necessary qualifiers and completed the refund form (if necessary), mail this material to the address shown on the refund form. This address is in many cases actually the address of a clearinghouse. A clearinghouse is an agency employed by the manufacturer to process all the refund offers. The clearinghouse also reimburses the retailers for redeeming the coupons, which is eventually paid for by the manufacturers. Two major clearinghouses in Canada are A. C. Nielsen Company of Canada Ltd. and Herbert A. Watts Ltd.

The clearinghouse ensures that the requirements for the refund offer have been complied with and confirms that the correct qualifiers have been enclosed. They, then, send the cheque, cash or replacement coupon out to the consumer within four to six weeks. REPLACEMENT COUPONS are coupons you receive in exchange for sending in proofs of purchase.

One advantage of the Smart Shopping system is that employed alone it can bring substantial savings to your budget. It can function quite independently of couponing and refunding and still save you time and money. However, used in conjunction with coupons and refunds, the savings are bountiful. Savings of about $20.00 per week or about $1,040 per year, depending on the size of your family, can be expected. The potential exists for a skilled shopper to earn even more.

To use all three elements you work a "Triple Play." For example, if you buy a bottle of a new liquid dishwasher soap normally priced at $5.49 on special for $3.19 with a $1.00 coupon, your total cost at this point would be $2.19. In addition the $1.00 coupon also doubled as a refund offer for $1.50 in coupons. Therefore, the total cost would be $2.19 less the $1.50 in useable coupons for more dishwasher soap.....value of savings $4.80. Actual cost to you for the dishwasher soap is 69 cents.

Procter and Gamble is the number one refunder in Canada. Other manufacturers who refund on a regular basis are:

Alberto Culver
Beatrice Foods Co.
Best Foods
Borden Inc.
Bristol Myers
Campbell Soup Co.
Colgate Palmolive
Del Monte
Frito Lay
General Foods
General Mills
Gillette
Green Giant

H.J. Heinz Company
Hunt Wesson
Johnson and Johnson
Kellogg's
Kimberley Clark
Kraft Ltd.
Lever Bros.
Nabisco Brands Ltd.
Pillsbury
Quaker Oats
Raltson Purina
Thomas J. Lipton
Warner Lambert Co.

Refund or rejection

It is not unusual for the following situation to arise. The consumer has submitted a form to the Box Number specified on the refund offer and for some reason the refund is not received by return mail. Why not? There are several good reasons for the delay and they are as exasperating for the clearinghouse as they are for the refunder. You may be about to receive your first "rejection letter", instead of a refund. The letter could read like this:

Dear ....

Your request for a refund for the offer as advertised has been returned due to an oversight or misunderstanding of the requirements of the refund offer: Sunlight Refund. Since there are thousands of consumers responding to refund offers at any one time, we must be fair to all who request the refunds and ask that you adhere to all the specified requirements.

Your request for a refund is being returned to you for any of the reasons listed below. Please feel free to re-submit your corrected refund request and we shall be happy to process it.

Form requested and not enclosed. (Store, newspaper, magazine).

No proofs of purchase enclosed.

Cash register tape not included.

Number of proofs of purchase not sufficient.

Please send .... more.

A re-submission of your refund request can only be accepted if the following does not apply:

Exceeded limit of one per household, family, groups as specified on form.

Offer expired.

Other.

Yours sincerely,

Also, the clearinghouse will usually return your qualifiers with the letter. To avoid a rejection letter, follow the requirements of refund offers precisely. Occasionally a company will accept an incorrect qualifier. For example, if you were required to send in two inner seals from a 750 ml jar of peanut butter and you submitted proofs for 500 ml jars, the company would rather you had bought the larger jars, but may accept your refund request since you have met the primary objective - bought the product.

If you should, after all your efforts, receive a rejection letter, forge ahead, undaunted, there are many more fish to be caught in the refunding sea.

Refund records

If you are an avid refunder and send out refund requests on a regular basis, you may want to keep a record of what you have submitted so that you have the necessary information should you need to track down a refund that has gone astray. Not too many refunds are lost in the mail, either coming or going. If the consumer has a legitimate complaint about a lost refund, the clearinghouse will usually gladly re-issue the refund as soon as they are notified of the problem.

The usual waiting period is about 4 to 6 weeks from time of mailing. If you have not received your refund within a week after the six week deadline has passed, you should write to the clearinghouse, clearly stating the following:

- your name;

- your address, including your postal code;

- the refund to which you originally responded;

- its value;

- the company offering the refund;

- and the qualifiers you submitted.

Any and all information that you can supply to the clearinghouse will be instrumental in either locating your original material or simply replacing the refund.

Name of Refund	Address	Value	Forms	Mailed	Received
ACTIFED Empty Carton CRT/Price Circled	P.O. Box 6069, Paris, Ontario N3L 3T2	$2.00 Cash	FR/NI	5/5/87	7/8/87
CARNATION 8- UPCs from 385 ml size of Carnation Evaporated Milk	P.O. Box 6028, Paris, Ontario N3L 2T2	$1.00 cpn. for store eggs, butter or sugar	FR/SF	2/12/87	3/30/87
FIVE ROSES Red Triangle Unbleached flour	P.O. Box 9661, St. John, N.B. E2L 4M8	$1.00 Cash	FR/HM	5/15/87	6/30/87
TASTER'S CHOICE Complete Hang tag form	P.O. Box 8025, Oshawa, Ontario L1H 8K7	$1.00 x 3 coupons	FR/HT	1/15/87	2/20/87
Please Note: The above refunds have all expired and are for illustration only.					

Refund record chart

If another week or two should elapse and you still have not received an answer from the clearinghouse, write directly to the company which offered the refund giving all the necessary information. Usually this will not be necessary as clearinghouses are prompt in replying to refund requests and are also very efficient. Keeping a record of your refund requests is not only valuable in tracking down a request that appears to have gone astray, but, also, it enables you to evaluate at a glance how much you have earned. It is possible to earn hundreds of dollars through refunding. Obviously the more brand name products you use, the greater the chance you have of being able to cash in on the savings offered.

Refund newsletters

How does the average consumer become aware of all of the hundreds of refund offers being made available each year? The best way is to subscribe to a refund newsletter. Scouring the supermarkets, newspapers, magazines and products for offers can be very time consuming. A refund newsletter does it all for you in one neat package. The usual subscription rate is less than $10.00 per year for six issues ...... well worth the money.

Refund newsletters inform you of refunds currently available, their expiry dates, limits, nature of the refund offer and where to send your request for a refund. They may also contain refund tips and information which can turn a rookie refunder into an expert.

They will also include a classified ad section in which you can give fellow refunders details of trades you wish to make. Some refunders will trade refund offer forms for cents-off coupons or premium coupons. Others will offer complete trade deals: i.e. form and qualifiers, and still others offer to trade qualifiers. Always enclose a self-addressed stamped envelope when replying to these ads.

By subscribing to a refund newsletter, it can help you touch bases with other people who, like yourself, are very interested in saving as much as possible, as often as possible.

According to Susan Samtur in "Cashing in at the Checkout," the very first refund newsletter was issued by Niles Eggleston about twenty-five years ago. How things have changed since the first issue hit the press! Consumerism has come to the fore over the years, more and more budget conscious shoppers are determined to save and earn as much as possible. Many refund newsletters have cropped up over the past few years, bringing valuable information about refunds, exchanges, round robins, contests and give-aways. The following is an example of what information found in a newsletter might look like:

EGGO WAFFLES REFUND OFFER: P.O. Box 2280, Station A., Toronto, Ont., M5W 1T3. Receive $1.30. Send in 3 UPC's from Eggo Waffles, any flavour. FR/SMP. Exp. March 31, 1987.

SUNLIGHT LIQUID REFUND OFFER: P.O. Box 504, Thornhill, Ont., L3T 6J7. Receive $2.00. Send 3 fronts labels from any size Sunlight Dishwashing Liquid. FR/SF. Exp. Feb. 28, 1987.

DEL MONTE/PINEAPPLE REFUND OFFER: P.O. Box 9467, Saint John, N.B., E2L 4X2. Receive $1.00. Send the UPC from any 2 cans of Del Monte Peaches, Pears, Fruit Cocktail or Pineapple. FR/Joy of Baking Calendar. Exp. June 30, 1987.

LIBBY'S DEEP-BROWNED BEANS CASH REFUND: P.O. Box 8024, Oshawa, Ont., L1H 8X7. Receive $2.00. Send 8 UPC's from any variety 14 oz. or 19 oz. Libby's Deep-Browned Beans. FR/HT. Exp. Feb. 28, 1987.

* ALL REFUNDS WERE TAKEN FROM THE CANADIAN SHOPPER MAGAZINE, FEB. 1987 ISSUE. ALL REFUNDS HAVE EXPIRED.

Listed below are some of the abbreviations you are likely to encounter in refund newsletters.

c/mo   cheque or money order
c/o   cents-off-coupon
COTL   Cash on the line
CPN   Coupon
CRT   Cash register tape
DM   Direct mail
ECI   Egg carton insert
EPOP   Each pay own postage
Exp.   Expires
FR   Form required
hdf   Hand drawn facsimile
h/f   Handling fee
HM   Home mailer
HT   Hang tag
LSASE   Large self-addressed stamped envelope
MF   Magazine form
n/a/p Name/address/phone number
NED   No expiry date
NF   Newspaper form
NFR   No form required
NI   Newspaper insert
NL   (no limit-send for offer as often as you wish)
PI   Package insert
POP   Proof of purchase
ppp   Plain piece of paper

rhdf   Reasonable hand-drawn facsimile
SASE Self-addressed stamped envelope
SF   Store form
SMP   Specially marked package
UPC   Universal Product Code
WSL   While Supplies Last
1-4-1   One for one, equal value trade

All good newsletters should contain the following:

1) a detailed list of which refund offers are currently available that require forms and their expiry dates;

2) a secondary list of refunds offered that require no forms, and their expiry dates;

3) a list of refunds with no expiry dates and no forms;

4) separate listing of "specially marked packages" refund offers and all other pertinent information

5) abbreviations used in the newsletters

6) a section on items that can be obtained free of charge

7) a section of manufacturer offers on products at reduced prices

8) a section of offers from manufacturers on items you can acquire with some proof of purchase material and some cash.

9) a classified ad and swapping information section

Giveways

How do you get the mailman to bring you gifts — for practically nothing? The smart consumer takes advantage of give-aways, and premium offers. In the past you could "buy" donut makers, T-Shirts, tote bags, electric razors, colouring books, hats and toys, to name just a few, all by just using your qualifiers saved from national brand products.

Basically there are four types of manufacturer's giveaways:

1) FREE: The most common type of "freebie" is the sample. Manufacturers give away small samples of their products in stores and via home mailers to introduce their products or expand their markets for established products. Sometimes you will receive a sample in the home-mailer along with a coupon for the product as well. There also exists the two-for-one coupon whereby you purchase two cans of a product to earn one can free.

2) ALMOST FREE: These gifts are considered almost free because you must submit some proofs of purchase in order to receive your gift. Offers of this type could be a free soup mug from Campbell's or a free calendar from Starkist's Nine Lives.

3) CASH PLUS: This type of offer requires the participant to send in certain qualifiers plus money to receive the "giveaway". For example, for $9.00 and two complete individual wrappers from Dial Soap, you would receive a shower radio. Another type of cash plus premium is the "point system". The consumer saves various proofs of purchase which have been assigned designated points printed on the packaging. Luvs Disposable diapers offered a baby track suit for $7.00 plus 12 proof of purchase points. The different packages of diapers earned you different points.

All offers have expired.

[8] A Marketer's Guide to Consumer Refunds, A.C. Nielsen Company of Canada Ltd., 1987, Pg. 6.
[9] A Marketer's Guide to Consumer Refunds, A.C. Nielsen Company of Canada Ltd., 1987, Pg. 11.

From this day forward — Amen!

People's attitudes as to what constitutes a "home cooked" meal, have been altered by their hectic lifestyles: their own and their children's. More and more after school and after work activities mean that family members do not always sit down together at the table every night. Today, even more often than not, a home cooked meal is one that is prepared in the home, but not necessarily from scratch.

In discussions with many women who work outside the home, the age old guilt feeling of not making a meal from scratch has eased somewhat. Making this compromise means more time can be spent with the children as opposed to time spent in the kitchen. Manufacturers, too, have responded to the needs of their consumers who have demanded fast, tasty, nutritious and economical meals. The frozen food section of the supermarket is no longer merely a place for ice cream and frozen juices, pizza and popsicles. Walking down an aisle of the frozen food department in today's supermarket is akin to looking at a menu in a restaurant.

Long gone are the days of TV dinners being served in emergencies or when Mum and Dad went out for dinner. The dinners are still available, but so, too, is a panorama of other delicacies to tempt your palate.

For singles, of all ages, the supermarket is an ideal place to shop for gourmet products which do not require a lot of preparation. For working mothers, these products offer a sensible alternative for nights when cooking from scratch just does not work out.

The products run the gamut from frozen meat pies, seafood entrees and frozen entrees, to vegetables in pastry, to name only a few. For a better selection, visit your local supermarket.

The beauty of these products in my opinion, is that they are the next best thing to FRESHLY made meals. Because they are frozen right out of the manufacturer's oven, no additives or preservatives are necessary to preserve freshness or taste. All products are clearly labelled so that where MSG has been used to enhance flavour, you are so informed.

In addition to the usual frozen fare, you will find a good selection of frozen vegetables. It is my belief that flash frozen vegetables, especially in Canada during the winter, are preferable to fresh food hauled over long distances. Food fresh from greenhouse outlets really is fresh. When you consider how much of the produce we consume during the winter months, is trucked here from far away countries, it cannot always be considered to be at its peak of freshness. In spite of rapid air transportation, many of the items are picked several days prior to reaching the stores.

However, when vegetables and fruits are flash frozen, they are usually processed within hours of harvest, helping to ensure optimum freshness. I found a wonderful company which sells flash frozen fruit and vegetables: MacMillan Orchards with outlets in Whitby and Acton, Ontario. The quality is excellent and the variety superb. I particularly like the fact that I can buy the vegetables in 5 lb boxes, full of product which can be scooped out easily. Look for a similar kind of operation in your province. The value can be exceptional.

Supermarkets also cater to workers who are tired of brown bagging their lunch. A quick survey of large retail chain supermarkets shows that salad bars are available, with a selection as good or better than some restaurants. As well, in the produce section you will find individual portions of some vegetables for singles to make their own salad at home. The A&P chain, for example, has a single portion policy which allows you to buy any amount of product. (I admit, you cannot buy just one Oreo cookie!)

In-store delicatessen sections are now the "in" thing in many chains. Singles, young, middle-aged and mature shoppers can drop in on their way home and pick up just what they feel like having for dinner. There is, therefore, no need for them to stand in long checkout lines. This helps eliminate the need to decide before leaving for work what you want to have for dinner 12 hours later.

Fresh fish, seafood and shellfish, now making an appearance at the fresh fish counters, indicate that the retail chains are responding to the demand for more fish. We can buy shark steaks, fresh salmon, squid, crab meat and many other delectable varieties.

One major Ontario chain recognized the need for leaner beef, in keeping with society's trend toward a diet containing less fat. The chain purchased a large supply of lean beef from a specially raised herd of cattle in Alberta. Marketing boards for both beef and pork have made great strides in reducing fat content in their products.

A major dairy launched a low fat 1% milk in Quebec and Manitoba in 1987. This milk tastes and looks just like 2%, but is in between skim milk and 2% in fat content. This product is a great boon to consumers who are watching their weight, women who want to increase their calcium consumption without the extra fat, children with weight problems and seniors who also wish to drink milk without increasing fat intake.

In the late 1970's, stir-frying became the easiest and fastest method of cooking for one or many, using little or no fat. By cooking with a little fat, usually olive oil, over high heat, you mostly sear the meat and steam the vegetables in minutes.

Pasta and potatoes became popular again. When people realized it was what you PUT ON the food NOT the FOOD itself, which increased the caloric content, the two foods came back into vogue.

For the most part, suburbanite families frequent supermarkets. Downtown families tend to use markets and Delis. They may venture to suburbia to stock up on paper and household products. Not to forget the singles, of all ages, childless couples and seniors, who, too, must shop and who frequent, mostly, the recently emerging super Delis which may be open for business, seven days per week.

One of the many concerns for this group, is how to shop effectively without throwing out more than they eat. I do not know many people who know just what they want to eat for dinner at 6 a.m. You have an unexpected luncheon appointment or you get home later from work than expected. In many cases you are too tired to attempt the ambitious meal you had planned. As a result, the fish you chose in the early hours of the day ends up in the garbage bin.

Because there is an abundance of Delis and speciality shops either in the area where you work or on your way home, picking up dinner (not fast food) is possible. In this way, you can decide on the spur of the moment what it is you would like to eat for supper that night. There are other advantages too...you buy only what you need and no more.

You can afford more expensive cuts of meat because you are only buying one or two pieces. All your fruits and vegetables, as well as bakery products, will be fresher. By the time you make a salad or cook the vegetables, your main course will be ready. Stir-frying or microwave cooking are fast and easy methods of cooking and cleaning up afterwards.

Dining alone is not the most pleasurable event. Many of us were nurtured on family dinner gatherings with conversation and later lingering over coffee and dessert. Too often, singles and seniors find the chore of cooking for one to be daunting.

In the event that you are forced to dine alone on a regular basis, take the trouble to make it "special" for you alone. Always use a nice place mat, cloth napkin and candles. If possible, avoid watching television, although it does provide some company. Instead, play your favourite music and sit back and enjoy your meal. Reading at the table, while enjoyable, does not allow you to fully concentrate on the task at hand ... eating. In some cases, after the meal is finished, you do not feel mentally satisfied as you have little or no recollection of eating. This can lead to snacking later. The same holds true when people stand at the kitchen counter and eat. There seems to be a lack of perception of having eaten a "real meal". Mums tend to do this when their children are little. Nibbling on leftovers while waiting for their spouse to come home for dinner can add many pounds. One suggestion is to have your salad with your children and then eat the main meal with your husband.

It does not matter where you shop or when (following previously set guidelines), as long as you try to do a good job. Keep in mind that many large retail chains are now offering 24 hour service which enables the shopper to pick a time suitable to his or her schedule. For singles or seniors, specialty shops and Delis, might just be right, with personal service they might enjoy and appreciate.

We are blessed, especially in the larger communities, with almost an endless variety and selection of different types of shops in which to make wise food selections. Take advantage of those which suit you, your lifestyle and your menus. It might mean spending a little more per pound to avoid throwing out twice as much unused food, purchased for less.

A recent survey conducted by Ruston/Tomany and Associates on behalf of Foodland Ontario, during the summer of 1987, produced some interesting information. According to Cheryl Creet, Public Relations Coordinator for Foodland Ontario, Ontario's cooks are still getting out their recipes and heading for the kitchen in order to feed their family and friends. "Surprisingly, the study showed that six out of seven main family meals are still prepared and eaten in the home", said Cheryl, "and the use of recipes continues to flourish."

The survey identified four "cooking types". These were determined more by lifestyle, attitudes and habits than by demographics such as education, income and age.

The four types, according to the survey's findings, are:

MAINTENANCE COOKS -Stick to tried and true recipes
INNOVATIVE COOKS &
OUTGOING GOURMETS -Most likely to try new recipes

CAREER URBANITES   -Little time for meal preparation

Approximately half of all Ontario's cooks use recipes at least once a week, primarily for home entertaining and special occasions.

"Consumers are most likely to prepare a dish if it contains ingredients that are fresh and readily available and if it is quick and simple to prepare," noted Cheryl, and "there's a marked preference for ingredients consumers are familiar with and use regularly."

While many of the results gleaned from the survey's findings are specifically reflective of the Ontario experience, some of the facts can be extrapolated across the country. By and large, it would appear (based perhaps on wishful thinking of my own) that many of us still find time to make a meal from scratch several times a week and to even introduce something new once in a while.

Movies, travel, "California trends" and books are but a few of the influences, according to Bonnie Stern, famous for The Bonnie Stern School of Cooking, which have a direct affect on what we eat. Health oriented foods are still popular. Consumers still enjoy their desserts, but opt for high quality. Personally, if I am going to indulge, the calories consumed have to be worth every single bite. Also, the dessert has to be worth the extra work-out necessary to burn off the calories the next day!

The one prediction I have heard, which I find very interesting, is that the style of meals for some will change to a variety of smaller appetizers rather than consuming one large meal. Personally, I already opt for this kind of evening meal if I have had a generous lunch.

Microwave ovens are becoming increasingly popular. With over 40% of all Canadian households possessing a microwave, fast and simple meal preparation becomes possible. A new product for use in the microwave came to Canada in 1986. Parchment paper, once used by our grandmothers in their daily baking, is now used by many cooks in their microwave. The paper can be re-used, does not require venting and is strong enough to be used in the freezer as well. In addition, it is a boon to the person who enjoys baking. I like it because the cookie sheet or pizza pan never gets dirty, eliminating the need to wash up afterwards. The paper can be found in your local grocery store, either in the paper section or in the bakery aisle. Some of the brand names which you might encounter, listed alphabetically are: Baker's Mate, Cook's Delight, Kitchen Parchment and Serla Bake.

Whether you eat a full meal, or a small one, have something delectable or something to just stave off the pangs of hunger, you have to eat. How, when, what and where you decide to eat will be entirely your choice. However, in the final analysis you will eat. Bon Appetit!

"Bad men live that they may eat and drink, good men eat and drink that they may live." SOCRATES

Recipes to Tempt Your Palate

The survey conducted for Foodland Ontario found that "approximately half of all Ontario cooks use recipes at least once a week. These recipes are sourced from personal collections, cookbooks, magazines, newspapers and brochures".

During five years of my weekly appearances on Global T.V.'s News at Noon program, my viewers regularly requested copies of the recipes demonstrated on the show. Each segment received an average of 400 requests from my many regular viewers, some from as far away as the southern United States. The response rose to 2000 requests for special seasonal recipes. I was repeatedly asked to produce a selection of these recipes and this I have now done.

Of the over 1,000 recipes used, I have tried to select the most popular ones. My favourite sources for recipes are Canadian Living, Chatelaine, Recipes Only, Foodland Ontario and The Ontario Milk Marketing Board. Some of the recipes printed here are from these publications (as acknowledged), while many others are ones I have collected over the years. They are all delicious. Newspapers are also excellent sources of good recipe ideas.

It's as Easy as Apple Pie...(If you follow the recipe)

A very dear friend of mine, who shall remain nameless, (so that she remains a friend) invited me over for lunch. Many years ago, when our children were very young, we initiated a ritual of treating ourselves, on occasion, to a fancy lunch at home. This eliminated the need for sitters, transportation and spending a great deal of money. We were also able to practise our culinary skills (or lack thereof).

On this particular occasion, my hostess had served a sumptuous lunch, saving the best for last! A beautiful strawberry cheesecake appeared on the table. It was not until I attempted to swallow the morsel I had chosen, when I discovered my mouth full of undissolved gelatin. You have no idea how awful that glutinous mass tasted and felt. In order for you to truly appreciate the comedy of the situation, I shall relate it to you verbatim:

Guest (that's me):	What is in this cake?
Mrs. No-Name:	I couldn't get the gelatin to mix in with the yogurt.
Guest:	Did you not dissolve it first in cold water, heat over boiling water, allow it to cool and then add to the yogurt?
Mrs. No-Name:	Was I supposed to do that?
Guest:	What did the recipe say?
Mrs. No-Name:	Oh, I couldn't be bothered following the recipe. I just did it the way I THOUGHT it should be done!

The cheesecake was scraped into a blender, puréed, strained and PRESTO, with a little prayer, it became strawberry yogurt and quite edible too! The crust was dispensed with. GARBAGE! All for the want of taking the time to read the recipe.

The moral of the story is obvious. Take the time to follow the instructions. First get out all the necessary equipment and ingredients. If you follow the steps precisely, you will avoid wasting time and food.

In addition, please do not be daunted by a "long" recipe. This same friend, admitted to me, that in the olden days, she never attempted a recipe that was over a certain length. In many cases, while it may appear to be overly long, it is often just a very carefully explained recipe which is really quite simple to follow. As long as you can read, have all the ingredients and equipment at your ready, you can accomplish anything.

Saving the Best 'Til Last

By rights, desserts and special treats should appear last in this section. I know as well as you do, that the first section you are going to look for is this one. Desserts still hold a special attraction for all of us with a sweet tooth. I have, therefore, decided to be a bit unorthodox (after all it is my book) and get the most delicious and sweetest dishes out of the way first. Enjoy!

Strawberries Romanoff

1 quart	strawberries
3 oz	Frangelico
3 oz	Grand Marnier
3 oz	Drambuie
1 pint	whipping cream, whipped
2 cups	vanilla ice cream, (softened)

Mash half the quart of strawberries. Pour liqueurs over the berries and let soak for several hours. Just before serving, add softened ice cream and whipped cream. Stir well to mix. Add sliced strawberries. Pour into tall wine goblets. Delicious!

(I always buy the small 2 oz bottles of liqueur, especially if it is a flavour I do not normally buy. This makes the dish more affordable).

The expression says it all

Lime Apple Cheesecake

2 cups	applesauce, strained to remove any excess liquid
1 cup	fine graham cracker crumbs
2 tbsp	brown sugar
1/4 cup	butter, melted
1/4 cup	finely chopped pecans
1 tall can	evaporated milk, (1 7/8 cups)
1 package	lime jelly powder, (3 oz)
1 envelope (1 tbsp)	unflavoured gelatin
3/4 cup	boiling water
1 package	cream cheese, (8 oz), softened
3/4 cup	granulated sugar
2 tsp	grated lime rind
1/2 cup	coarsely chopped pecans

Heat oven to 350°F (180°C). Have ready a 9 inch springform pan. Combine wafer crumbs, brown sugar, butter and finely chopped pecans. Press firmly into the bottom of the springform pan and half an inch up the sides. Bake for 5 minutes and then cool.

Pour evaporated milk into a metal pan and place in the freezer to partially freeze. This will take about 30 minutes. Meanwhile, combine jelly powder and unflavoured gelatin. Add boiling water and stir until gelatin is dissolved. Cool but do not chill. Cream cheese and sugar together until smooth and fluffy. Stir in 2 cups of applesauce, cooled gelatin and lime rind. Set in ice water and chill until the mixture begins to set. Beat mixture with electric beater, adding chilled evaporated milk gradually. Continue beating until very light and fluffy. Pour over crumb bottom in pan. Sprinkle with coarsely chopped pecans. I usually decorate just the edge. Chill for several hours, preferably overnight.

Crumb Cake

A very special lady, Josephine Bell, first introduced me to Crumb Cake many, many years ago. Every time I make it, I think of my very dear friend. The aroma created as the cake bakes brings back fond memories of sitting at her pine kitchen table in her home at Base Petawawa. Mrs. Bell's table was a place where, as teenagers, we were allowed to carve our names and the date we first sat at the table for a special treat from her kitchen. We also carved hearts and initials of our current loves. This is her recipe.

1	egg
1/4 cup	butter
1 cup	buttermilk
1 1/2 tsp	all-purpose flour
1 tsp	soda
1 tsp	baking powder
1 tsp	cinnamon

Crumbs:

Mix the following ingredients together to make a crumb mixture.

1 cup	brown sugar
1/4 cup	butter
1/2 cup	all-purpose flour

Cream the butter, add sugar, beaten egg, then add the sifted dry ingredients alternately with the milk and vanilla. Pour the batter into an 8 inch square greased and floured cake pan. Sprinkle the crumbs lightly over the top. Bake in a 350°F (180°C) oven for 45 minutes. This is delicious on its own or with vanilla ice cream.

Deep Dish Apple Pie

Pastry for 1 crust pie

2 lb	tart cooking apples
1 tbsp	lemon juice
1 cup	granulated sugar
3 tbsp	all-purpose flour
1/2 tsp	nutmeg
1/4 tsp	cloves
1	egg yolk
1/2 cup	whipping cream

Prepare pastry. Refrigerate, wrapped in parchment paper for later use.

Pre-heat oven to 400°F (200°C). Lightly grease 1 1/2 quart casserole. Wash apples; pare; core; slice thinly into a large bowl. Sprinkle with lemon juice. Combine sugar, flour and spices; gently toss with apples, mixing well. Turn into prepared casserole. On a lightly floured surface, roll out pastry into a 9 1/2 inch circle. Fit over top of casserole; flute edge. Make several cuts, 1 inch long in centre, for vents. Brush lightly with egg yolk beaten with 1 tbsp of water; bake for 50 to 60 minutes. Top should be golden brown and apples tender. Remove from oven to rack. Pour cream into vents.

Peach Kuchen

I had the privilege of living in Germany for several years. One of the favourite treats for my sister, brother and myself, was to go downtown on Saturday with Mum and have tea and kuchen in a quaint little German coffee house. I do not have words to accurately describe the taste of this dessert. You simply must try it yourself. Be prepared to become addicted to it.

Boiling water

2 lb	ripe peaches, peeled and sliced
2 tbsp	lemon juice

Kuchen Batter:

1 1/2 cups	all-purpose flour
1/2 cup	granulated sugar
2 tsp	baking powder
1/2 tsp	salt
2	eggs
2 tbsp	milk
1 1/2 tbsp	grated lemon peel
1/4 cup	butter, melted

Topping:

1/4 cup	granulated sugar
1/2 tsp	ground cinnamon
1	egg yolk
3 tbsp	whipping cream

Sweetened whipped cream or soft vanilla ice cream

Pre-heat oven to 400°F (200°C). Pour enough boiling water into a large bowl to cover the peaches. Let stand 1 minute to loosen skins. Then plunge in cold water for a few seconds. With a paring knife, pare peaches, place in a large bowl. Then slice. Sprinkle peaches with lemon juice to prevent darkening. Toss to coat with lemon juice. Set aside.

Sift flour with the sugar, baking powder and salt onto a sheet of parchment paper. In a large mixing bowl, using a fork, beat eggs with milk and lemon peel. Add flour mixture and melted butter, mixing with fork until smooth, about 1 minute. Do not over mix. Butter a 9 inch springform pan or a 9 inch round layer cake pan.

Turn batter into pan. Spread evenly over the bottom. At this point the kuchen can be refrigerated for several hours or until about 1/2 hour before baking.

Combine sugar and cinnamon; mix well. Drain peach slices. Arrange on batter, around edge of pan, fill in centre with 5 peach slices. Sprinkle evenly with sugar-cinnamon mixture. Bake 25 minutes. Remove kuchen from oven. With a fork beat the egg yolk with the cream. Pour over peaches. Bake 10 minutes longer. Cool 10 minutes on wire rack. To serve, remove side of springform pan.

(If you have used a cake pan, serve directly from the pan). Serve kuchen when warm. Cut into wedges and top with sweetened whipped cream or soft vanilla ice cream. Makes 8-10 servings.

Orange Chocolate Mousse

4 oz	semi-sweet chocolate, chopped
3	eggs, separated
6 tbsp	softened butter
1 tbsp	orange liqueur
1/2 tsp	vanilla extract

Place the chocolate in a saucepan. Set the saucepan in hot, almost boiling water and cover. Let melt over low heat. Remove the pan from the heat and beat the egg yolks one at a time into the hot chocolate until the sauce thickens slightly. Beat in the butter, orange liqueur and vanilla extract. Leave to cool slightly. Beat the egg whites until stiff. Stir a quarter of the egg whites into the chocolate mixture, and then gently fold this mixture into the remaining egg whites. Let cool completely. Decorate mousse with a sprig of fresh mint if you wish.

(Recipe courtesy of Recipes Only, February 1986, Page 32, Issue 14).

Chocolate Lemon Frozen Cream

1/2 cup	granulated sugar
Rind of 1 lemon	
3 tbsp	water
1/2 tsp	vanilla
1 cup	whipping cream, whipped

Chocolate Part:

3 tbsp	melted butter
1 cup	chocolate wafer crumbs
1/4 cup	brown sugar
1/4 cup	chopped nuts

Stir the sugar, rind of 1 lemon and 3 tbsp of water, over low heat until the sugar is melted. Remove from the heat and add the vanilla. Let stand until cold. Add whipped cream.

Mix all of the remaining ingredients until well blended. Put half the chocolate mixture in a loaf pan lined with foil. Cover with cream mixture. Sprinkle with remaining crumbs. Freeze. This is divine. It is my Mum's recipe and she always made two because one was never enough.

Kahlua Mocha Mousse

1/2 cup	Kahlua
1/2 cup	dark créme de cacao
3/4 cup	strong brewed coffee
Instant decaffeinated coffee granules	
1 cup	icing sugar
1/4 tsp	almond extract
1 envelope	unflavoured gelatin
7	egg yolks, beaten
7	egg whites
2 cups	whipping cream, whipped
2 tbsp	icing sugar
Finely chopped pecans	

In the top of a double boiler, combine Kahlua, créme de cacao, brewed coffee, 3/4 tsp coffee granules, 1 cup sugar, extract, gelatin and egg yolks; mix well. Cook over boiling water (do not let water touch the bottom of the pan) stir until mixture thickens, (10 to 15 minutes).

Meanwhile, fold a 26-inch piece of waxed paper lengthwise into thirds. With a string, tie this paper around a 1 quart soufflé dish to form a collar 2 inches high. When coffee mixture is thick, remove from heat and set top of double boiler in a bowl of ice cubes.

Let coffee mixture stand, stirring occasionally, until mixture thickens and mounds when dropped from a spoon. Meanwhile, in a large bowl, beat egg whites with electric mixer at high speed until stiff peaks form when beaters are lifted; set aside.

In a medium bowl, beat 1 1/2 cups whipping cream until stiff. Using a wire whisk, fold coffee mixture and whipped cream into beaten egg whites, using an under and over motion. Turn mixture into the prepared soufflé dish. Place in the refrigerator and chill for several hours or overnight.

Before serving: In a chilled bowl, combine 1/2 cup whipping cream with 2 tbsp icing sugar. Beat until stiff peaks form. Spoon into pastry bag fitted with number 6 star tip. Take soufflé dish from refrigerator; remove and discard paper collar. Pipe whipped cream decoratively into swirls around top edge of mousse. Sprinkle cream with more coffee granules and press finely chopped pecans around edge.

(Recipe courtesy of Kahlua).

The Great Pumpkin Cookie

4 cups	all-purpose flour, unsifted
2 cups	quick oats, uncooked
2 tsp	baking soda
2 tsp	ground cinnamon
1 tsp	salt
1 1/2 cups	butter, softened
2 cups	firmly packed brown sugar
1 cup	granulated sugar
1	egg
1 tsp	vanilla extract
1 can	pumpkin, (16 oz)
1 cup	chocolate chipits

Pre-heat oven to 350°F (180°C). Combine flour, oats, soda, cinnamon and salt. Set aside. Cream butter, gradually add sugars, beating until light and fluffy. Add egg and vanilla; mix well. Alternate additions of dry ingredients and pumpkin, mixing well after each addition. Stir in chipits. For each cookie, drop 1/4 cup of dough (yes, one quarter of a cup) onto lightly greased cookie sheet or one lined with parchment paper. Bake at 350°F (180°C) for 20 to 25 minutes until cookies are firm and lightly browned. Remove from cookie sheet and cool on racks.

NOTE: DO NOT USE PUMPKIN PIE FILLING

Kahlua Truffles

12 ....1 ounce squares semi-sweet chocolate (375 g)
4 ....egg yolks
1/3 cup ....Kahlua
2/3 cup ....unsalted butter
Cocoa (unsweetened)
Ground almonds

Melt chocolate in top of a double boiler (or zap in a microwave). Remove from heat, cool to room temperature. Add yolks, one at a time, stirring constantly until thoroughly blended. Mix in Kahlua; return to simmering water for 2 to 3 minutes, stirring constantly. Pour mixture into bowl of electric mixer. Beat in butter, a table-spoon at a time. Continue beating mixture until it is fluffy in texture. Cover with plastic wrap; refrigerate for 4 to 5 hours or overnight. Roll into 3/4 inch balls; then roll balls in bitter cocoa or nuts. Refrigerate until ready to use. Yields 3 dozen.

Kahlua and Fresh Fruit

1 1/2 quarts................fresh fruit such as melons, berries, pineapple, kiwi fruit, oranges, grapes
3 tbsp ....brown sugar, packed
3/4 cup ....Kahlua

Combine fresh, chilled fruit, cut into bite-sized pieces. Add brown sugar, sprinkled over fruit. Add Kahlua. Mix gently. Cover and refrigerate 30 minutes. Serve with a sprig of mint.

Kahlua Chocolate-Dipped Strawberries

2 oz. ....semi-sweet chocolate
1 tbsp ....Kahlua
1 tsp ....unsalted butter
8 ....whole fresh strawberries

In a double boiler, combine chocolate, Kahlua and butter. Dip strawberries in the Kahlua chocolate mixture and place on parch-ment paper. Refrigerate 30 minutes.
(Recipes courtesy of Kahlua).

Audrey's April Fool

```
1 pint ........................fresh strawberries or kiwi fruit
1/4 cup ......................honey
Pinch salt
3/4 cup ......................whipping cream
```

Hull or peel fruit. Blend with honey and salt until smooth. Whip cream until soft peaks form. Fold in fruit mixture. Serve in wine glasses with ladyfinger cookies.

Chocolate Rum & Raisin Cheesecake

There is no way to describe this dessert other than to say it is positively decadent. It is so delicious that it will leave you speechless. (Friends, who know me well, will tell you that it takes a lot to make Rhonda speechless). This cheesecake does just that. It has become the preferred Christmas dessert at our house. Make it often, eat it often and enjoy it always.

```
1/4 cup ......................raisins
1/4 cup ......................rum or 1 1/2 tsp rum extract in 1/4
                             cup water
1 1/4 cups..................graham cracker crumbs
1/4 cup ......................granulated sugar
1/3 cup ......................butter, melted
3 ...............................eggs, separated
2 cups .......................milk
2 envelopes................unflavoured gelatin
1 tbsp .......................instant coffee granules
3 oz...........................semi-sweet chocolate chips
3 packages.................cream cheese, (8 oz each), softened
1/2 cup ......................granulated sugar
```

Soak raisins in rum or rum extract; set aside. Combine graham crackers crumbs, sugar and butter; press firmly into the base of a 9 inch springform pan; refrigerate. Beat together egg yolks and milk, sprinkle in gelatin and whisk to combine. Stir constantly over low heat until gelatin dissolves and mixture thickens, about 5 to 10 minutes. Add coffee and chocolate chips; continue stirring over low heat until melted and smooth; remove from heat. Beat cream

Making a dumpling into a chef.

cheese and sugar until light and fluffy; gradually beat in gelatin mixture, raisins and rum. Chill until mixture mounds slightly when dropped from a spoon. Beat egg whites until stiff but not dry; fold into gelatin mixture. Pour into springform pan; chill until set, about 2 to 3 hours. When set, decorate with chocolate curls and sprinkle with icing sugar if desired. Makes 6 to 8 servings.

(Recipe courtesy of The Ontario Milk Marketing Board, Milk Calendar, 1983).

Making Dumplings into Chefs

Granted it takes the patience of Job to allow little helpers into the kitchen. But I have always been a firm believer in letting my three children, of various ages, "help" me make something. My parents always encouraged my siblings and me to acquire expertise in creating culinary delights. Whether the help consists of "dumping and stirring", lining the muffin or cupcake tins, rolling out the dough for a pie or licking the bowl and beaters, it provides fun and a learning experience for little ones. Ramsey, my six year old, received a chef's hat, apron and oven mitts, as a gift — all designed for "playing" at being in the kitchen. Ramsey took it to heart, and now dons his "uniform" whenever he catches me baking. I am not sure whether more flour ends up on Ramsey, me or the floor. In any event, all three children help out, not just in the baking sessions. Ryen is now an expert at peeling potatoes and carrots (never onions, that's Mummy's job) and Ijade makes wonderfully creative salads.

Granola Cookies

3/4 cup	vegetable shortening
3/4 cup	brown sugar
1	egg
1/4 cup	water
1 tsp	vanilla
1 cup	graham flour
1 tsp	salt
1/3 tsp	baking soda
3 cups	granola

Pre-heat oven to 400°F (200°C). Beat shortening, sugar and egg together. Blend in water and vanilla. Sift flour, salt and soda together. Add to the creamed mixture. Beat well. Add granola and stir to mix. Drop small amounts on cookie sheet lined with parchment paper. Bake at 400°F (200°C) for 10 to 12 minutes.

Lucy's Home Run Cookies

Ramsey, my son, was helping me make these cookies one Sunday afternoon. As we were waiting (Mummy patiently and Ramsey impatiently) for the first batch to come out of the oven, my little helper offered this suggestion. "Mum, I know a way to make things easier for you so that making cookies will not take so much of your time," he said as he tried to sneak a spoonful of batter from the bowl. I waited for him to go on. "Don't you think it would be easier if you just made the batter and let us eat it right out of the bowl? That way you would not have to go to the trouble of baking all these cookies. So, what do you think about that idea Mum?" (All said with a look of perfect innocence on his cherubic face!) "But Ramsey", I said, "you would miss out on the lovely smell of the cookies baking, as well you would have difficulty taking one to school for a snack". A concerned look passed over his face. "Okay Mum, we'll do it your way for now," as he once more attempted to scoop up some of the batter.

I'm not sure which is more fun, making cookies for them or with them. One thing I know for sure, they must be good, because when I go to get one to enjoy with my cup of tea, they are always gone.

2	medium bananas
2 cups	granola
1 1/2 cups	all-purpose flour
1 cup	packed brown sugar
1 tsp	cinnamon
1 tsp	baking powder
2	eggs
1/2 cup	margarine, melted
1/4 cup	oil
1 cup	chocolate chips

Pre-heat oven to 350°F (180°C). Peel and slice bananas into a blender. Whirl until puréed. Combine granola, flour, sugar, cinnamon and baking powder. Mix well. Stir in bananas, eggs, margarine and oil. Fold in chocolate pieces. Place 1/4 cup of batter onto a greased baking sheet or one lined with parchment paper. Press batter into 2 1/2 inch to 3 inch wide cookies. Bake at 350°F (180° C) for 17 minutes or until lightly browned. Yields 18 to 20 cookies.

Yogurt Dessert

1 package	flavoured gelatin, (3 oz)
1 cup	boiling water
2 1/2 cups	plain yogurt

Take any flavour of gelatin. Mix with boiling water. Stir until powder is dissolved. Add yogurt and stir well. Put into individual dessert dishes. Lemon is especially good served with fresh, sliced strawberries. Apricot is divine when sprinkled with sliced toasted almonds. (I think small children can assist in making this dessert as long as you handle the boiling water for them).

Pineapple Delight

This dessert is so simple to make and so very, very good. My Aunt Dorothy introduced this recipe to our family many years ago. It has now become a family favourite. With all the whipped cream, icing sugar and butter it can be considered a bit sinful, but worth every bite. What is very nice about this recipe, is that the children can do it by themselves.

2 cups	graham wafer crumbs
1/2 cup	soft butter
1 cup	icing sugar
2	eggs
1/2 cup	chopped nuts
1 can	crushed pineapple, (20 oz), drained
1 cup	whipping cream

Place half the crumbs in an 8 inch square pan. Blend butter and icing sugar until light and fluffy. Add eggs one at a time, beating well after each addition. Spread mixture over crumbs. Sprinkle with nuts and pineapple. Whip cream to peaks and spread on top of pineapple. Cover with remaining crumbs. Chill at least 4 hours.

Strawberries/Honeydew Melon Balls

Hull and wash one quart of strawberries. Clean out the seeds of a honeydew melon and use a melon baller to make small balls. Pour cream over fruit. Sprinkle with a small amount of cinnamon. Serve chilled.

Crunchy Peach Halves

Daddy just loves ice cream. In particular, he loves butterscotch ripple ice cream. Daddy always asks for a serving of ice cream, and then promptly falls asleep, thus letting it melt. Yech! who wants warm ice cream? In any event, Daddy says it is because the cold ice cream hurts his teeth. We all think it is because he likes to snooze after dinner in his big recliner. At least this dessert provides him with a genuine reason for liking melted ice cream.

1 can	peach halves, (14 fl.oz)
1/2 cup	walnut pieces
2 tbsp	brown sugar
1 tbsp	soft butter

Butterscotch ripple ice cream

Place peach halves on a broiler pan and place under the broiler after you have filled the halves with nuts and sprinkled sugar over the top. Then add a dollop of butter to each half. Broil until sugar and butter are melted and bubbling. Remove from oven and place each peach half in a dessert dish. Top with a generous scoop of ice cream.

Blueberry Upside Down Cake

2 tbsp	butter
1/2 cup	brown sugar
2 cups	blueberries
3	egg yolks
1 cup	granulated sugar
1 cup	all-purpose flour
5 tbsp	milk
1 tsp	baking powder
1/2 tsp	salt
3	egg whites

Whipped Cream

Melt butter in the bottom of an 8 x 8 x 2 inch pan. Sprinkle with brown sugar. Add berries. Beat yolks and stir in sugar. Beat in flour, milk, baking powder and salt. Beat egg whites until stiff. Fold into

Daddy and his ice cream,
both at room temperature.

cake batter. Pour batter over fruit. Bake at 350°F (180°C) for 45 minutes. Loosen edges and turn out onto platter for serving. Cut into squares and serve with whipped cream.

Butterfly Treats

Spread either cream cheese or cheese spread on pieces of bread. Cut out circles with biscuit cutter. Place two pieces of mandarin oranges on the bread rounds with the inner curved part facing outward. (These make the wings.) Then place a strip of date between the two orange sections to complete the butterfly.

Raisin Faces

Spread cheese spread or peanut butter on circles of bread and make faces with raisins. Then cut the bread into different shapes with a cookie cutter. This is easier to do after you have spread the cheese or peanut butter. Handling the small shapes is both difficult and messy.

Crunchy Peanut Butter Balls

1/4 cup	liquid honey
1/2 cup	crunchy peanut butter
1/2 cup	skim milk powder
1/2 cup	uncooked rolled oats
1/4 cup	coarsely ground walnuts

Blend together the first four ingredients. Grease hands with margarine or butter. Use 1 tsp of the mixture for each ball. Roll in the palm of your hand to make a small ball. Roll in chopped nuts. Makes 2 to 3 dozen balls if made by an adult who does not nibble during the manufacturing process. The children just love making and eating these and therefore the yield may be lower.

I'd rather be in bed!

Starting the Day Off on the Right Foot

There are two kinds of people who you may encounter first thing in the morning. They are the grumps or the bright spirits. While I fall into the latter category, my nine year old son Ryen, if left to his own devices, would probably rather still be asleep at 9:30 in the morning.

The bright spirits bounce out of bed at first light, spring down the stairs, start the coffee perking, set the table, make freshly squeezed orange juice and pancakes from scratch, all in 10 minutes. The grumps, by comparison, do not know what they want to eat in the first place, don't care in the second place and would much rather be back in bed, thank you very much!

My other two children, Ijade and Ramsey, are very much like me and manage to squeeze in "Good morning" right before "What's for breakfast, Mum?"

Whether you like breakfast or grimace at the sight and smell of food so early in the day, you will find something just right for you in this section. Yes, Puffy Peach Pancakes with Ice Cream, or a pizza or quiche are okay for breakfast once in awhile.

MMMMMUFFINS!

They just have to be the best way to start the day, especially if you do not like to eat a heavy meal early in the morning. Fresh out of the oven, along with a hot cup of coffee and a slab of creamy butter — just the way I like them and so will you!

I like to make up the dry ingredients separately the night before. I even line the muffin tins. I set the oven on the automatic timer to pre-heat the oven before I awaken. In the morning, when I come "springing" down the stairs, all I have to do is to mix the wet with the dry ingredients and put the muffins in to bake. By the time the heavenly aroma has wafted through the house, the children are ready for breakfast, just as the timer dings.

Banana Peanut Butter Muffins

2	eggs, lightly beaten
1/2 cup	honey
1/2 cup	vegetable oil
1 cup	mashed banana
1/2 cup	peanut butter, crunchy or smooth
1 tsp	vanilla
1 1/2 cups	all-purpose flour
1 tbsp	baking powder
1/2 tsp	baking soda
1/2 tsp	salt

Pre-heat oven to 400°F (200°C). In a large bowl, combine eggs, honey, oil, banana, peanut butter and vanilla. (If peanut butter seems oily, you may wish to cut down the oil to about 1/3 of a cup. If you want to reduce the calories in the muffins, reduce the oil to 1/3 of a cup and increase amount of mashed banana to 1 1/2 cups, to add moisture). In a second bowl, mix flour, baking powder, soda and salt. Add to egg mixture and stir until just combined, about 10 to 20 seconds. Spoon mixture into 10 greased or paper-lined muffin tins; filling them about 2/3 full. I sometimes use custard cups to give the muffins the "muffin shop" look. Bake until just lightly browned, about 20 minutes. Remove from pan and cool on rack.

Apple Cheddar Muffins

2	eggs, lightly beaten
1/4 cup	honey or maple syrup
1/4 cup	vegetable oil
1/2 cup	buttermilk or yogurt
1 cup	grated old Cheddar cheese
1 cup	cake flour
1/2 cup	whole wheat flour
1 tsp	ground cinnamon
1 tsp	ground allspice
1 1/2 tsp	baking powder
1 1/2 tsp	baking soda
1/2 tsp	salt
1 cup	peeled, chopped apple

Pre-heat oven to 400°F (200°C). In a large bowl, combine eggs, honey, buttermilk, oil and cheese. In a second bowl, mix cake flour, whole wheat flour, spices, baking powder and soda and salt. Add to egg mixture, stirring just until well combined, about 10 to 20 seconds. Fold in apple. Spoon mixture into 10 buttered or paper lined tins, filling about 2/3 full. Bake until lightly browned, about 20 minutes. Remove from pan and cool on rack.

(Recipe courtesy of Foodland Ontario).

Spicy Rutabaga Muffins

2	eggs
1 cup	rutabaga, cooked and mashed
2/3 cup	milk
1/4 cup	vegetable oil
2 1/4 cups	whole wheat flour
3 tsp	baking powder
1/4 tsp	salt
1 tsp	cinnamon
1/4 tsp	ground nutmeg
1/4 tsp	ground cloves
1/2 cup	brown sugar

Pre-heat oven to 400°F (200°C). Beat eggs in a medium bowl. Add rutabaga, milk and oil. Mix well. Combine all remaining ingredients and stir into rutabaga mixture. Spoon into 12 greased muffin cups. Bake at 400°F (200°C) for 20 to 25 minutes. This recipe is a terrific way to use up leftover rutabaga or to make for children who say they do not like rutabagas. What they don't know won't hurt them!

(Recipe courtesy of Ontario Foodland).

Blueberry Orange Muffins

2 1/2 cups	all-purpose flour
3/4 cup	granulated sugar
2 tsp	baking powder
1/2 tsp	salt
1/2 cup	butter
1 cup	orange yogurt
2	eggs, lightly beaten
2 tsp	grated orange rind
1 1/2 cups	fresh blueberries

Pre-heat oven to 400 F (200 C). In a large bowl, mix together flour, sugar, baking powder, baking soda and salt. Cut in butter until mixture resembles fine crumbs. In a small bowl, combine yogurt, eggs and orange rind. Add to flour mixture all at once. Stir until just combined. Gently fold in blueberries.

Divide batter equally among 12 large greased custard cups. Bake in 400 F (200 C) oven for 20 minutes, or until done. Serve warm with butter.

Savory Muffins

4	eggs, lightly beaten
1/2 cup	vegetable oil
1 can	condensed cream of celery or mushroom soup, (10 oz)
1 cup	celery, finely chopped or mushrooms, finely chopped
1/4 cup	grated Parmesan cheese
2 tbsp	fresh parsley, chopped
1/2 tsp	celery salt
1/4 tsp	garlic powder
1 tsp	onion powder
2 cups	all-purpose flour
2 tbsp	baking powder
1 tsp	baking soda

Pre-heat oven to 400°F (200°C). In a large bowl, combine eggs, oil, undiluted soup, celery, cheese, parsley, celery salt, garlic and onion powder. In a second bowl, mix flour, baking powder and soda. Add to egg mixture and stir until just blended. Spoon mixture into 12 buttered and paper-lined tins, filling about 2/3 full. Bake until lightly browned, about 20 minutes. Remove from pan and cool on rack. Serve with tomato soup or meat loaf.

Carrot Prune Muffins

3	eggs
1/3 cup	brown sugar
1/2 cup	molasses
2/3 cup	vegetable oil
1 cup	chopped prunes
2 cups	natural bran
1 cup	shredded carrots
1/2 cup	wheat germ
2 cups	all-purpose flour
2 tsp	baking powder
1 tsp	baking soda
1 tsp	salt
1 1/4 cups	milk

Pre-heat oven to 375°F (190°C). Beat together eggs and sugar. Stir in molasses and oil. Add prunes, bran, carrots and wheat germ. Sift together flour, baking powder and soda, along with the salt. Add the dry ingredients alternately with the milk. Fill lined muffin tins 2/3 full. Bake at 375°F (190°C) for 20 minutes.

Blueberry Bran Wheat Germ Muffins

3	eggs
1 cup	brown sugar
1/2 cup	oil
2 cups	buttermilk
1 tsp	vanilla
1 cup	wheat germ
1 cup	bran
2 cups	all-purpose flour
2 tsp	baking powder
2 tsp	baking soda
1/2 tsp	salt
1 1/2 cups	blueberries

Pre-heat oven to 400°F (200°C). Combine the wet ingredients and the dry separately. Then mix the wet and the dry together in a large bowl. Fill the lined or greased muffin tins 2/3 full. Bake at 400°F (200°C) for 20 to 25 minutes.

Orange Oatmeal Muffins

1 cup	rolled oats, regular or quick cooking
1/2 cup	orange juice
1/2 cup	boiling water
3	eggs, lightly beaten
1/2 cup	margarine or butter at room temperature
1/2 cup	brown sugar
1/3 cup	granulated sugar
1 cup	all-purpose flour
1 tsp	baking powder
1 tsp	baking soda
3/4 tsp	salt
1/4 tsp	nutmeg
1 tsp	vanilla
1 cup	raisins

Pre-heat oven to 350°F (180°C). In a small bowl, soak oats in orange juice and water for 15 minutes. In a large bowl, cream together butter and sugars. Beat in eggs and oat mixture. Blend flour, baking powder and soda, salt and nutmeg together. Stir into batter. Stir in vanilla and raisins. Spoon batter into greased or paper-lined muffin tins, filling them about 2/3 full. Bake until golden brown, about 20 minutes. Makes 16 large muffins.

Apple and Oatmeal Muffins

1 1/2 cups	all-purpose flour
1 tbsp	baking powder
1/2 tsp	baking soda
1/2 tsp	salt
1 tsp	cinnamon
1/2 tsp	ginger
Pinch Allspice	
1/2 cup	oats, quick cooking or rolled
1/2 cup	firmly packed brown sugar
1 1/2 cups	apples, diced and peeled
1	egg, lightly beaten
1 cup	milk
1/2 cup	melted butter or margarine

Pre-heat oven to 400°F (200°C). In a bowl combine flour, baking powder, baking soda, salt and spices. Stir well. Stir in rolled oats and sugar. In separate bowl combine apples, egg, milk and butter. Add to dry ingredients; stir just until combined. Spoon batter into muffin tins lined with paper baking cups, filling them level. Bake in 400°F (200°C) oven for 20 to 25 minutes. Makes 12 muffins.

(Recipe courtesy of Foodland Ontario).

Zucchini Muffins

4	eggs
1 cup	granulated sugar
1/2 tsp	vanilla
1 cup	vegetable oil
2 cups	grated unpeeled zucchini
3 cups	all-purpose flour
1 1/2 tsp	baking powder
1 tsp	baking soda
1 tsp	salt
1 tsp	cinnamon
1 tsp	nutmeg
1 tsp	allspice

Pre-heat oven to 375°F (190°C). With electric mixer, beat eggs with sugar and vanilla for 2 minutes. Gradually add oil and beat 2 minutes longer. Blend in grated zucchini. In large bowl, combine flour, baking powder, baking soda, salt and spices. Blend well. Add liquid mixture to dry ingredients and using a wooden spoon, stir until just moistened.

Spoon batter into muffin tins lined with paper baking cups; filling each to the top of the paper liner. Bake at 375°F (190°C) for 25 to 30 minutes.

Good morning! Muffins

Children, unlike some of the adults I know, take recipe instructions literally. A friend tells the story of how her son, then aged ll, was discovered busily making muffins from a mix. Frances wandered into the kitchen to discover Jason, up to his elbows in muffin mix busily mixing the batter. His hands were buried deep in the muffin mixture. When questioned as to "what he was up to?" the very serious and straight forward reply was immediate: "Mum, the instructions said —"and mix by hand." Who said children don't read instructions carefully?

1 1/2 cups	raisins
1/2 cup	butter
3/4 cup	brown sugar
1/2 cup	molasses
4	eggs
2 cups	milk
2 cups	bran
2 cups	whole wheat flour
1 tsp	baking powder
1/4 tsp	baking soda
1/2 tsp	cinnamon
1/2 tsp	nutmeg
Dash salt	

Pre-heat oven to 400°F (200°C). Place the raisins in a bowl. Cover with boiling water and let sit. Cream together the butter, brown sugar and molasses. Add eggs one at a time. Beat until well blended. Add milk all at once. Mix together bran, flour, baking powder, soda and spices. Add all at once and stir until just blended.

Add raisins. Spoon into muffin tins lined with paper or well-greased, 3/4 full. Bake at 400°F (200°C) for 18 to 20 minutes.

The Most Important Meal of The Day

For those of you who like a more substantial breakfast you might find something that suits your fancy on the next few pages.

Following recipe instructions to the letter.

Raisin Bread

```
1 cup ........................... raisins
1/2 cup ...................... lukewarm water
1 tsp ........................... granulated sugar
1 pkg ........................... dry active yeast
1/2 cup ...................... scalded milk
2 tbsp ......................... granulated sugar
1 1/2 tsp ................... salt
1 tsp ........................... cinnamon
2 ................................. eggs, slightly beaten
2 tbsp ......................... soft butter
3 1/2 cups ................. all-purpose flour
Melted butter
Sugar
```

Cover raisins with boiling water and let stand 5 minutes. Drain well. Measure lukewarm water into mixing bowl. Add 1 tsp sugar and stir to dissolve. Sprinkle yeast over water and let stand 10 minutes. Stir well. Cool scalded milk to lukewarm add to yeast mixture along with 2 tbsp sugar, salt, cinnamon, eggs and soft butter. Add half the flour and beat well with a wooden spoon.

Add raisins and enough of the remaining dough to make the dough easy to handle. Mix thoroughly with your hand. Turn out onto a floured surface and knead until smooth and elastic.

Round up the dough into a ball and place in a greased bowl, cover with a damp cloth and let rise until doubled in bulk, about 1 1/2 hours. Punch down dough and let rise again for 30 minutes.

Shape into a loaf and place into a greased 9 x 5 x 3 inch loaf pan. Cover and let rise for about 45 minutes. Heat oven to 400°F (200° C). Brush loaf with melted butter and sprinkle with sugar. Bake for 30 to 35 minutes until lightly browned on the top. Makes one loaf.

Omelette Chatanuga

Prepare a standard omelette. Before folding omelette over, fill with some of the sauce. (See recipe below). Fold omelette over, pour remaining sauce over entire omelette.

1/2 cup	sour cream
1	small green pepper
1/4 tsp	dill salt
1	medium tomato, cut into small wedges

Heat sour cream and dill salt. Quickly and gently stir in green pepper and tomato pieces. Heat through, but do not boil.

Zucchini Bread (AKA Breakfast Bread)

I first tasted this bread at my sister Randy's home. Until I tried it, I was not convinced that it would be as good as she claimed. I was pleasantly surprised. I forgot about the recipe until this past summer. I had planted four zucchini plants in my little garden and, much to my amazement, they grew to be quite healthy and large. I was then faced with the problem of what to do with them. Neither my children nor I really like cooked zucchini and there was far too much for me to eat raw. (Why, you are asking yourself, did she plant it in the first place? The reason, it turns out, was to make zucchini bread and muffins). The children, however, who just devour these loaves of "bread" do not know what they are really eating. One evening I made a double batch of the recipe while the children were outside playing. Upon entering the house they exclaimed as to what was that wonderful aroma emanating from the oven. I quickly answered "breakfast bread". To this day, (unless of course they actually read Mummy's book) they still love to eat it and believe it is breakfast bread.

1/2 cup	chopped nuts
1/2 cup	chopped date
3 cups	all-purpose flour
1 tsp	baking soda

```
1 tsp ............................baking powder
3 tsp ............................cinnamon
3 ..................................eggs
2 cups .........................granulated sugar
1 cup ...........................vegetable oil
3 tsp ............................vanilla
2 cups .........................grated zucchini
```

Combine dry and wet ingredients. Add grated zucchini and mix. Pour into greased loaf pans. Bake 1 hour at 350°F (180°C). Makes 2 loaves. This recipe can be easily doubled. Freezes well.

Skier's Breakfast

```
6 ..................................eggs
1/4 cup .......................thinly sliced ham or flakes of ham
1/2 cup .......................mild cheese (Gouda or Swiss)
Salt
Paprika
Butter
```

The night before, break the eggs into a 9 inch pie plate. Each egg should have enough room to spread out. Top with sliced ham and cheese. Sprinkle with spices and dot with butter. Cover with plastic wrap and place in refrigerator. In the morning place the dish in a 350°F (180°C) and bake until the egg whites are set. Serve with toast or tea scones found on page 150.

Cheese and Bacon Surprise

```
Sliced whole wheat bread or English muffins
Sliced Cheddar cheese
Slices of ripe tomatoes
Strips of bacon
```

Butter one side of bread or English muffin. Place one slice of cheese on top. Cover cheese with tomato slice. Criss cross two slices of bacon over the top of the tomato. Place under pre-heated broiler until bacon is tender crisp and cheese is melted.

Bran Bread

2 cups	all-purpose flour
1 tsp	baking soda
1 cup	brown sugar
2 cups	buttermilk or sour milk
2 cups	bran
1 cup	raisins
1/2 cup	chopped nuts or dates

Pre-heat oven to 350°F (180°C). In a large bowl, sift flour, soda, salt, and brown sugar. Stir in milk and mix well until ingredients are combined. Fold in bran, fruit and nuts. Pour into a greased 9 x 5 inch pan. Bake at 350°F (180°C) for 60 minutes. Keeps well without freezing.

Breakfast/Supper Quiche

For families with members who do shift work, devising a meal suitable for everyone to share in the wee hours of the morning is not difficult when you consider serving quiche. For the person arriving home, its becomes dinner with a salad, but for the person just leaving for work, it is breakfast. I even encourage the children to eat pizza for breakfast. It provides all the basic essentials in dairy, meat, vegetables and breads that you require. It is not, in my opinion, junk food.

1	9 inch quiche or deep pie plate lined with unbaked pastry
1	large onion, chopped
1/2 cup	mushrooms, sliced
1/2 tsp	oregano
3/4 tsp	salt
1/2 tsp	garlic powder
1/4 tsp	marjoram
1/4 tsp	pepper
2 tbsp	butter
1 package	cream cheese, (4 oz)
1/2 cup	Parmesan grated cheese
1 cup	milk
3	eggs, beaten

1 cup ....broccoli, chopped and cooked
1/2 cup ....soft bread crumbs
4 ....tomatoes

Pre-heat oven to 425°F (220°C). Sauté onions, mushrooms and seasonings in butter. Cream cheeses together ; blend in milk. Add beaten eggs. Fold in broccoli, bread crumbs, onions and mush-rooms. Pour into pastry lined shell. Arrange tomato slices around outer edge. Bake at 425°F (220°C) for 10 minutes. Lower tem-perature to 350°F (180°C) and bake for 25 minutes longer. Test with knife to ensure the quiche is set. If not, cook for another 10 to 15 minutes at 350°F (180°C). Let stand 10 minutes before serving.

Peameal Bacon Quiche

1 ....9 inch pie plate lined with unbaked pastry
1 package ....frozen asparagus or 8 fresh stalks
1/2 lb. ....peameal bacon, cut into 1/4 inch cubes
1 ....large onion, thinly sliced
1 cup ....1/4 inch cubes of Swiss cheese
4 ....eggs
1 1/2 cups ....light cream
1/4 tsp ....dried savory
1/2 tsp ....salt
1/4 tsp ....pepper
1/4 tsp ....oregano
Pinch fresh dill

Pre-heat oven to 450°F (230°C). Have ready 9 inch pie plate lined with pastry. Build fluted edge to hold in filling. Cover the edge with narrow strip of parchment paper to prevent excess browning. Put in oven for 5 minutes (do not prick bottom.) Remove from oven and cool.

Cook asparagus until tender crisp. Drain very well. Cut into 1/2 inch pieces. Cook slices of peameal until lightly browned. Put well drained pieces of peameal into pie pan. Cover with sliced onions. Add cheese cubes and asparagus. Beat eggs and cream together with a fork. Stir in seasonings. Pour over meat and vegetables in pie plate. Bake for 15 minutes at 450°F (230°C). Turn down heat to 350°F (180°C) and continue baking for another 30 to 40 minutes or until knife comes out clean. Serve hot.

Seafood Quiche

1	9 inch pie shell, unbaked
1 cup	shredded Mozzarella cheese
1/3 cup	onion, finely chopped
4	eggs
2 cups	half and half cream
3/4 tsp	salt
1/4 tsp	pepper
1//8 tsp	cayenne pepper
1 can	crab meat
1 can	baby clams
1 can	shrimp

Pre-heat oven to 425°F (220°C). Prepare pastry. Sprinkle crab meat, which should be well drained, over pie shell along with cheese and onion. Beat eggs slightly; beat in remaining ingredients. Pour egg mixture over other ingredients in pie plate. Cook uncovered at 425°F (220°C) for 15 minutes. Reduce temperature to 300°F (150°C). Cook uncovered until knife inserted in centre comes out clean, about 30 minutes. Let stand 10 minutes before cutting.

Blender Breakfasts

Honey Grapefruit Flip: Whisk together 1/2 can or 1/3 cup of frozen grapefruit juice with 3/4 cup milk, 2 eggs and 1 tablespoon of honey.

Hawaiian Treat: Whirl together 1/2 cup pineapple juice with 1/2 cup milk and a ripe banana. Add an egg if you like. You can also make this drink with 1/2 cup pineapple, 1/2 cup milk and 1/2 cup peaches.

Spiced Apple Chaser: Whisk together 1/2 cup apple juice, 1/4 cup plain yogurt, 1 egg and a sprinkling of cinnamon.

Raspberry Julep: Whisk together 1/2 package of frozen raspberries with 3/4 cup buttermilk and a dash of vanilla.

Pear Parfait: Peel pear and whirl with 1/2 cup buttermilk and a generous sprinkling of ginger.

Banana Orange

2 1/2 cups	milk
2	eggs
1	medium banana, quartered
2 tbsp	liquid honey
1/3 cup	frozen orange juice, thawed

Blend all the ingredients together and serve immediately. Great for breakfast or a pick-me-up during the day.

Fruit'n Eggnog Shake

3	eggs
1/4 cup	granulated sugar
2 cups	milk
1/2 tsp	vanilla
1 1/2 cups	fruit juice

Beat eggs with 1/4 cup sugar until well blended. Add milk gradually, stirring constantly. Cook in saucepan over medium heat, stirring constantly until mixture thickens. Stir in vanilla. Pour into pitcher and refrigerate overnight. Serves three. In the morning, pour 3/4 cup of eggnog shake into a tall glass and stir in 1/2 cup of fruit juice.

Fruit with Yogurt and Granola Topping

2 tsp	butter
2 tbsp	quick cooking oats
1 tbsp	wheat germ
1 tbsp	chopped nuts
1 tbsp	sunflower seeds
1 tbsp	brown sugar
1 tsp	cinnamon
1 tsp	allspice
2 tsp	natural bran
2 tsp	dried currants
2	peaches or plums or kiwi fruit, peeled and pitted or 1 cup of berries of your choice
1 cup	fresh plain yogurt

In a saucepan melt butter over medium heat. Add rolled oats, wheat germ, nuts, sunflower seeds, brown sugar, spices, bran and currants. Cook, stirring occasionally, for about 5 minutes, until mixture is lightly browned. Slice fruit into individual serving bowls, cover with yogurt and sprinkle with topping. This breakfast dish tastes best served when it is still warm. The topping can be made ahead and re-heated in the microwave.

Light as a Feather Pancakes

When I was a little girl, many moons ago, Sunday morning was special. It was the one day Daddy made breakfast. It always consisted of pancakes and sausages and they were always good. The tradition has been carried on in my home and the pancakes then, as now, are always made from scratch.

1 cup	all-purpose flour
2 tbsp	baking powder
2 tbsp	granulated sugar
1 cup	milk
1	egg
2 tbsp	vegetable oil

Combine flour, baking powder and sugar. Mix together milk, egg and vegetable oil. Add wet to dry ingredients. Mix thoroughly. Cook in pre-heated skillet. No fat is required, even for an ordinary frying pan. I use a 1/4 cup measure for each pancake.

Puffy Peach Pancake

When I first received a copy of this recipe from Foodland Ontario I raised a quizzical eye when I saw ice cream included. I found out very quickly that the children thought I was (and I quote) "THE GREATEST MUM IN THE WHOLE WORLD!" when I served it to them one summer morning. It has become standard fare in our home on Sunday mornings. So much so, I know the recipe by heart. (Actually, it helps to know it well, especially if I get to bed late on Saturday night). I have on occasion used apricots when peaches were not available.

```
1/4 cup ...................... butter
1/4 cup ...................... granulated sugar
1/4 tsp ....................... cinnamon
3 ............................... peaches, peeled and sliced
4 ............................... eggs, separated
1/3 cup ...................... granulated sugar
1/3 cup ...................... all-purpose flour
1/2 tsp ....................... baking powder
Dash Salt
1/3 cup ...................... milk
Sour cream or vanilla ice cream
```

Melt butter in a round 10 inch x 1 1/2 inch oven-proof dish or skillet. Sprinkle evenly with sugar-cinnamon mixture. Top with peach slices. Bake at 400°F (200°C) for 8 to 10 minutes.

Meanwhile, beat egg whites until foamy. Gradually beat in 1/3 cup sugar, until soft peaks form. Set aside. Combine flour, baking powder and salt. Blend into yolks and milk. Fold egg whites into yolk mixture. Spread evenly over peaches. Bake 20 minutes. Loosen edges, invert onto serving plate. Cut into wedges and serve with sour cream or ice cream.

(Recipe courtesy of Foodland Ontario).

Just two leeks and a speeding ticket!

Midday

Remember my No-Name friend on page 2. She's back with another story. Let me set the scene. It was a lovely May day. Mr. No-Name was home from work with a bad back. It was her turn to prepare our monthly lunch.

The first course was the delicious mushroom and leek soup which you will find on page 141. I had never had the occasion to use leeks and inquired as to the cost involved. The following conversation took place:

Guest (That's me again): Are leeks expensive to buy?

(Mrs. No-Name's face is very red).

Mr. No-Name: Not really, about $14.00. (You can imagine my shock).

Guest: $14.00? What do you get for that, a whole bushel?

Mr. No-Name: No, just two leeks and a speeding ticket!

As it happened, she had forgotten to purchase the leeks while shopping, remembered part way home, sped back to the store before it closed, which was imminent. The policeman was not sympathetic.

Lunch, in many countries is the big meal of the day. A lighter repast is then consumed in the evening. This makes a great deal of sense as it allows the body to digest the heavier meal while one is still active. We tend to repose after the dinner meal, causing the body to work harder to digest the food just eaten. However, North Americans still prefer to eat the lighter meal at noon. Included in this section are suggestions for light lunches, entertaining fare and creatively bagged lunches.

Banana Dog

1 ....whole wheat hot dog bun
1 ....banana
Peanut butter

Spread a generous amount of peanut butter on a hot dog bun. Wrap the bun in plastic wrap. Pack banana with bun in the bag. Your child will, then only, have to peel the banana and place it inside the hot dog bun, as you would do for a hot dog.

Cheese Dogs

Slice weiners down the middle, making about a 3 inch opening. Insert strips of your favourite cheese. Wrap the entire wiener in bacon and place under the broiler until bacon is tender crisp and cheese has melted. Serve in a bun.

Home Made Subs

1/4 cup ....mayonnaise
2 tsp..........................chili sauce
1 tbsp ....green onion, finely chopped
1/4 tsp ....chives, finely chopped
2 ....hard cooked eggs, chopped
Mini sub buns
Soft butter
1 ....small cucumber
6 slices......................cooked ham
6 slices......................Swiss cheese
1 ....large tomato, sliced paper thin
Salt and Pepper

Combine mayonnaise, chili sauce, green onion, chives and eggs. Cut subs in half. Butter both halves. Spread bottom half with a little of the mayonnaise and egg mixture. Add a layer of cucumber slices, a layer of overlapping ham slices, a layer of cheese slices and finally a layer of tomato slices. Sprinkle with salt and pepper. Spread with remaining mayonnaise mixture. Top with other half. Cut the two in half to serve. There should be enough sauce for about 3 subs. You could also serve this at home using a one pound French loaf.

Tote a Salmon Boat

2	large potatoes
1/2 cup	2% cottage cheese, well drained and mashed
1 tbsp	lemon juice
1 tsp	fresh parsley, chopped
1 can	salmon, drained and flaked
1/3 cup	celery, chopped
1/4 cup	green onion, chopped
Sprinkle garlic powder	
Salt and pepper	
1	tomato, cut into thin slices
1/2 cup	grated Cheddar cheese

Bake cleaned potatoes in a toaster oven at 425°F (220°C) for 1 hour or until done. Cool. Cut the potatoes in half and scoop out the pulp. Leave at least a 1/4 inch shell intact. Mash together potato pulp, cottage cheese, lemon juice and parsley. Stir in salmon, celery, and green onion. Season to taste with garlic powder, salt and pepper. Spoon mixture back into potato shells and place on a baking sheet. Bake at 350°F (180°C) for 20 to 25 minutes. Remove from the oven and top with 2 tomato slices and grated cheese. Return to oven for about 4 minutes or until cheese melts. If possible re-heat in the microwave at the office for 3 minutes on high.

Antipasto Salad

Salad:

1/2 lb	beans
12	small mushrooms
8 slices	salami
8 slices	cooked ham
1/2 cup	Mozzarella cheese cubes
4	hard cooked eggs, cut in wedges
1/2 cup	gherkin pickles
Leaf lettuce	

Dressing:

2/3 cup	vegetable oil
1/3 cup	red wine vinegar
1	garlic clove, minced
1 tbsp	chopped parsley
1 tsp	salt
1/2 tsp	basil leaves
1/2 tsp	oregano
1/8 tsp	pepper

Cook green beans in boiling water for 3 minutes. Rinse under cold water and drain well. Combine dressing ingredients in jar with tight-fitting lid. Shake well. Combine 1/4 cup dressing with beans and 1/4 cup with mushrooms. Cover and chill at least 30 minutes, stirring occasionally.

Arrange all salad ingredients attractively on lettuce on large platter. Serve immediately with remaining dressing.

(Recipe courtesy of Foodland Ontario).

Mediterranean Salad

A small child interested in helping out with dinner can tear up the lettuce for a tossed salad. Children can also be responsible for adding croutons and bean sprouts. When Ijade was four years old, she assisted me in making such a salad. Upon completion of the task, I started to put all the unused vegetables back into the refrigerator. Whilst my back was turned, Ijade decided to "toss the salad" just as she had seen me tossing it. The result was both disastrous and amusing. The salad ended up everywhere — her head and shoulders, the floor, the counter and even in the sink. There was very little left in the bowl. We both had a good laugh, cleaned up the mess and started over. Mum tossed the salad the second time around. Today, Ijade makes beautiful salads and now can toss them herself.

Salad:

1	small head Romaine lettuce cut into bite-sized pieces
1/2	cucumber, finely chopped
12	medium radishes, sliced
2	tomatoes, cut in wedges
1	small onion, sliced and divided into rings
1/2 cup	feta cheese cubes
1	carrot grated

Dressing:

1/2 cup	plain yogurt
1 tbsp	vinegar
1	garlic clove, minced
2 tbsp	milk
1/2 tsp	salt
1/8 tsp	pepper

In a bowl, combine salad ingredients, except feta cheese and carrot. Blend together dressing ingredients and pour over salad. Toss gently. Spoon cheese and grated carrot over top of salad. Serve immediately.

(Recipe courtesy of Foodland Ontario).

Tossing a salad with zest.

Hot'n Spicy Salad

1 lb	lean ground beef
1/2 cup	barbecue sauce
1/4 cup	sliced green onions
1 tsp	chili powder
1/4 tsp	salt
1/8 tsp	pepper
1	small head Iceberg lettuce, torn into bite-sized pieces
2	tomatoes, diced
1/2 cup	grated Cheddar cheese

In a frying pan, brown beef well. Drain off fat. Add barbecue sauce, green onions and chili powder. Simmer for 5 minutes, stirring occasionally. Divide lettuce on 4 plates. Top each with tomatoes. Spoon hot beef mixture over top of each. Sprinkle with cheese. Serve immediately.

(Recipe courtesy of Foodland Ontario).

Iced Strawberry Soup

1 quart	strawberries
1/2 cup	dry white wine
1/2 cup	water
1/2 cup	granulated sugar
1/8 tsp	allspice
1/8 tsp	nutmeg
1 cup	buttermilk

Wash, pat dry and hull strawberries. Set aside 8 for garnish. Purée remaining berries in a blender with wine and water. Pour into a large bowl. Stir in sugar, allspice, nutmeg and buttermilk. Chill 4 to 6 hours. At serving time, slice 8 remaining berries into soup. Makes 4 to 6 servings.

(Recipe courtesy of Foodland Ontario).

Mum's Potato Salad

6-8	potatoes
Vinegar	
1/4 cup	red pepper, chopped
1/4 cup	green pepper, chopped
1/2 cup	celery, chopped
4-6	hard boiled eggs, chopped
6-8	green onions, chopped
3/4 cup	mayonnaise
3/4 cup	sour cream
1 tsp	celery salt
1/2 tsp	pepper
3 tbsp	green relish
2 tbsp	table mustard
1 tsp	granulated sugar
1/2 tsp	salad dressing
1/2 tsp	paprika
1/2 tsp	garlic powder
1/2 tsp	marjoram, basil and thyme
1 drop Tabasco sauce	
Radishes to garnish	

Cook the potatoes in boiling water that has been salted and contains a glug of white vinegar. Cook potatoes until tender but not mushy. Drain and rinse in cold water. Mix together the green and red pepper, celery, eggs and onions. Blend the remaining ingredients together except for the radishes. Mix well and stir into potato and chopped vegetable mixture. Refrigerate overnight. Adjust seasonings to taste. Add more sour cream if desired. Garnish with radishes.

Chicken with Spiced Butter

2	chicken breasts or thighs, boned and skinned
1/4 cup	butter
1/2 cup	all-purpose flour
1 tsp	garlic powder

Spiced Butter:

1/3 cup	butter
1 1/2 tbsp	lemon juice
1 tsp	grated lemon rind
3 tsp	fresh gingerroot, finely chopped
1	green onion, finely chopped
1/4 tsp	salt
1/4 cup	fresh parsley, finely chopped

Cream butter and blend in lemon juice, rind, gingerroot, green onion and salt. Shape butter mixture into log about 1 inch in diameter and 3 inches long. Wrap in parchment paper and refrigerate for 30 minutes. Roll log in fresh parsley. Roll in new parchment paper and put into refrigerator.

In a skillet, melt butter. Dust chicken with flour spiced with garlic powder. Cook for about 7 minutes on each side until the chicken is cooked but not dry. At serving time, slice a round of the butter on the top of the hot chicken. The heat from the meat will melt the butter.

Ham Crepes with Cheese Sauce

Crepes and omlettes seem to be dishes which some people are leery of tackling. They really are quite easy. They can be made ahead of time and frozen. I place a piece of parchment paper in between each crepe prior to freezing. This allows me to take out as many or as few as I need. Crepes are really an elegant way to make a main dish offering for guests. (And yes, the first time I made them, I mangled the first two).

1 cup	cooked ham, diced
1/2 cup	mushrooms, sliced
3 tbsp	butter
3 tbsp	all-purpose flour
1 cup	milk
3/4 cup	grated Cheddar cheese

Crepes (recipe follows)

Melt butter in saucepan and heat until it bubbles up. Add flour all at once and stir until well blended. Cook, stirring occasionally, until thickened. Add Cheddar cheese and stir until cheese is melted. Cover and keep warm. Heat ham and mushrooms in saucepan. Add three-quarters of the cheese sauce to ham and mushroom mixture. Spoon into warm crepes. Fold edge over and cover with serving of cheese sauce. Sprinkle with chopped parsley. Serve hot.

Whole Wheat Crepes

2 1/2 cups	milk
4 tbsp	butter, cut up
1 cup	whole wheat flour
1 cup	all-purpose flour
1/4 tsp	salt
4	eggs, lightly beaten

Vegetable oil for frying

Warm the milk in a small saucepan with the butter. Set aside to cool slightly after the butter has melted. Put both flours into a large bowl. Add salt and mix by hand. With mixmaster running, gradually pour in milk and butter mixture. Add eggs and continue to beat until blended and smooth. Let stand for at least 30 minutes.

Brush a 6 inch crepe pan with a paper towel dipped into vegetable oil. Set over medium heat and heat until smoking. Pour 1/4 cup batter into the pan and immediately tilt and turn the pan so batter will cover the surface evenly. Turn the crepe when underside is well-browned, 3 to 4 minutes, and cook other side for 2 to 3 minutes. Slide crepe onto a piece of parchment paper. Repeat with remaining batter, stacking finished crepes; add additional milk if batter is too thick. Re-oil skillet after each crepe. When crepes are cool, use immediately or layer with parchment paper and freeze. Makes 16-6 inch crepes.

Mushroom and Leek Soup

1/2 cup	butter
1/2 lb	mushrooms, chopped
2	bunches of leeks
1/4 cup	all-purpose flour
1 tsp	salt
Dash cayenne pepper	
1 cup	chicken broth
3 cups	milk
1 tbsp	dry sherry

Wash leeks very well; slice and use white part only. In 1/4 cup of butter, sauté leeks until tender but not brown. Remove and set aside. In remaining butter, sauté mushrooms until soft — about 10 minutes. Blend in flour, salt and cayenne. Gradually stir in broth and milk. Cook, stirring until mixture thickens and comes to a boil. Add leeks, sherry, salt and pepper to taste. Simmer for 10 minutes. Serve with thin slices of lemon and a sprinkling of parsley.

(Recipe courtesy of The Ontario Milk Marketing Board, Milk Calendar, 1981).

Cucumber and Rice Salad

1 1/2 cups	water
1/3 cup	wild rice uncooked
1	English cucumber, diced
1	tomato, diced
1 1/2 cups	cooked chicken, diced
2	green onions, chopped
1/2 cup	radishes, sliced
2 tbsp	red wine vinegar
1/2 tsp	salt
1/2 tsp	dried oregano
1/4 tsp	pepper
2 drops	hot pepper sauce
2	garlic cloves, chopped
1/4 cup	olive oil

In a small saucepan, bring water to a boil. Add wild rice and return to boil. Reduce heat and simmer, covered 25 to 30 minutes. Drain.

In a large bowl, combine cucumber, tomato, chicken, green onions, radishes and wild rice. In a small bowl, blend vinegar, salt, oregano, pepper, hot pepper sauce and garlic. Slowly whisk in oil. Pour dressing over salad and toss. Chill 1 hour.

(Recipe courtesy of Foodland Ontario).

Chunky Cucumber Dip

1	English cucumber
1 package	cream cheese, (4 oz)
1/4 cup	mayonnaise
2 tbsp	fresh parsley, chopped
1 tbsp	lemon juice
1/4 tsp	pepper
Garlic	

Cut cucumber in half. Grate one half and slice remaining half. Place grated cucumber in a bowl. In second bowl, or in a blender, beat cream cheese, mayonnaise, chives, parsley, lemon juice, garlic and pepper. Use as little or as much garlic as you like. I used three large cloves. Drain cucumber. Add the balance of the ingredients and mix well. Chill for one hour. Serve with small pieces of pita bread or raw veggies.

(Recipe courtesy of Foodland Ontario).

Apple, Cheese and Pecan Salad

4	apples
Lemon juice	
1	celery stalk, cut in 1/2 inch pieces
1	small red pepper, cut into squares
2/3 cup	sharp or medium Cheddar cheese, cubed
1/2 cup	pecan halves
1/2 cup	mayonnaise
1/4 cup	plain yogurt
1/2 tsp	celery seeds
Freshly ground black pepper	
Lettuce leaves	

Core and cube apples; place in bowl, sprinkle with lemon juice and toss well. Add celery, pepper, cheese and pecans. Combine mayonnaise, yogurt, celery seeds and pepper to taste. Add to salad; tossing well. Cover and chill at least one hour before serving. If desired, serve on crisp lettuce leaves.

Strawberry and Spinach Salad

1 quart	strawberries
1 package	spinach or 1 head of lettuce torn into bite-sized pieces
1/2 cup	mayonnaise
1/2 cup	sour cream
1 tbsp	poppy seeds
1 tbsp	sesame seeds
1 tbsp	granulated sugar
1 tsp	lemon juice
1/8 tsp	ground ginger

Wash, pat dry and hull strawberries. Drain on paper towel. Slice. To make dressing combine all remaining ingredients, except lettuce or spinach. For each serving, place 1/2 cup lettuce or spinach on salad plate. Arrange 1/2 cup sliced strawberries on top, drizzle with 2 1/2 tbsp dressing.

(Recipe courtesy of Foodland Ontario).

Pizza Dough

1 tbsp	dry active yeast
1 1/2 cups	warm water
1/4 cup	dry skim milk
1 tbsp	coarse salt
1/4 cup	olive oil
2/3 cup	whole wheat flour
2 - 2 1/2 cups	all-purpose flour
Corn Meal	

Dissolve yeast in a large bowl in a 1/2 cup of the water. Stir in the dry milk and salt together with the rest of the water. Stir until dissolved, then pour over yeast. Add the olive oil, whole wheat flour, add about 2 cups of the all-purpose flour, stirring to mix. Then turn out onto a floured surface and let rest while you oil a large bowl.

Knead the dough until smooth, adding more flour as necessary — about 6 to 8 minutes. Return the dough to the bowl, cover with a clean cloth and let rise until doubled, about 1 hour.

Punch the dough down and divide into 2 pieces. (This will make 2-14 inch pizzas). Grease your pizza pan and start stretching the dough until it fits the pan. You can do this with your hands, easing it to fit. It will be bouncy and resistant, so you will have to work at it. Proceed making the pizza as outlined below.

Pizza with Pizzaz

Assemble all the ingredients you like on your pizza: green peppers, salami, mushrooms, tomato paste, mozzarella cheese, garlic powder, Parmesan cheese, onions, tomatoes, bacon, pepperoni, olives, anchovies, ham, pineapple — your choice.

Heat oven to 425°F (220°C). Grate cheese and sprinkle a small amount over the top of the pizza dough. Bake in the oven for 5 minutes. The cheese will seal the crust and prevent it from becoming soggy. Remove from the oven and spread a thin layer of pizza sauce over the melted cheese. Assemble your pizza as follows:

    layer of chopped vegetables
    sliced meat
    sliced mushrooms
    any extras
    garlic powder
    Parmesan cheese

Top with grated Mozzarella cheese. Then repeat layers until all ingredients are used up, but this time start with meat to prevent it from becoming overcooked on the top of the pizza. Press down with the flat of your hand to seal all the edges.

Bake at 425°F (220°C) for 25 minutes.

Tea Time

When Ijade and Ryen were very small, I had an occasion to invite a friend over for tea. I am afraid Avril was not prepared for what I had in mind. I had spent the better part of the morning baking all sorts of delectable goodies. Tea loaves, scones, home-made jam, bite-sized tea sandwiches, and cookies were all spread out on a large tray. She had expected a cup of tea and perhaps a cookie or two. My grandmother, Mabel, was born and raised in London, England, and I am therefore well versed in the art of having "tea". It is a lovely tradition, one that combines delicious food, a hot cup of tea and good friends. I have since had the pleasure of having tea at the King Edward Hotel in Toronto. If you check some of the better hotels in the downtown core of your city, you too might find a lovely place to have "a spot of tea." Failing that, use some of my recipes and enjoy your own tea time.

Tea Scones

2 cups	all-purpose flour
2 tbsp	granulated sugar
3 tsp	baking powder
1/2 tsp	salt
6 tbsp	butter
1	egg, slightly beaten
1/2 cup	milk

Pre-heat oven to 425°F (220°C). Sift together dry ingredients. Cut in butter until mixture resembles coarse meal. Add egg and milk, stirring until dough follows the fork around the bowl. Turn onto floured surface and knead gently 15 times. Cut the dough in half. Shape each half into a ball and either pat or roll the dough until it is about 1/2 inch thick and 6 inch in diameter. Cut into 8 wedges. Place on an ungreased baking sheet or sheet lined with parchment paper. Bake at 425°F (220°C) for 12 to 15 minutes. Makes 16. Serve piping hot with butter and jam.

Cheese Scones

2 cups	all-purpose flour
4 tsp	baking powder
1 tbsp	granulated sugar
1/2 tsp	salt
1/2 cup	shortening
3/4 cup	grated Cheddar cheese
3/4 cup	milk
1	egg, well beaten
2 tbsp	milk

Pre-heat oven to 425°F (220°C). In a large bowl combine flour, baking powder, sugar and salt. With a pastry blender, cut in shortening until mixture resembles fine crumbs. Stir in cheese. In a bowl, beat together 3/4 cup of milk and the egg. Add to flour mixture stirring lightly with fork until moistened. Turn dough onto floured surface. Knead gently 10 times. Roll pastry into circle about 1/2 inch thick. Place on ungreased baking sheet. Brush with 2 tbsp of milk. Score into 8 wedges but do not separate. Bake at 425°F (220°C) for 15 minutes or until golden brown. Makes 8 large scones.

Irish Soda Bread Biscuits

2 cups	all-purpose flour
1 tsp	baking powder
1 tsp	baking soda
1/2 tsp	salt
1/2 cup	butter
1/4 cup	fresh parsley, finely chopped
3/4 cup	buttermilk

Pre-heat oven to 450°F (230°C). Combine flour, baking powder, soda and salt. With pastry blender, cut in butter until mixture resembles coarse crumbs. Stir in parsley. Add buttermilk, stirring with fork to make soft dough.

Turn dough out onto floured surface and knead lightly about 10 times. Roll out to 1/2 inch thickness. Cut into 3 inch rounds. Place on an ungreased baking sheet. Bake at 450°F (230°C) for 12 to 15 minutes. Makes 12 biscuits.

Sourdough Biscuits

2 cups	all-purpose flour
1 tsp	baking powder
1/2 tsp	baking soda
1/2 tsp	salt
1/3 cup	shortening
1/2 cup	sourdough starter (See Following)
1/2 cup	buttermik

Pre-heat oven to 450°F (230°C). Mix the dry ingredients. With fingers, cut in shortening until mixture resembles coarse meal. Add starter and enough buttermilk to make soft dough. Knead lightly about a dozen turns on lightly floured surface. Then roll out to 1/2 inch thickness. With a biscuit cutter, cut desired size and place 1/2 inch apart on an ungreased cookie sheet. Bake at 450°F (230°C) for 10 to 12 minutes.

Basic Sourdough Starter

2 cups	lukewarm water
1/2 tsp	granulated sugar
1 pkg	dry active yeast
2 cups	all-purpose flour

In a non-metallic bowl, mix together water, sugar and yeast. Let stand for 10 minutes or until frothy. Gradually stir in flour until batter is smooth. Cover and let stand at room temperature for 2 to 3 days until bubbly and soured with a sharp, almost wine-like odour. Use immediately or store covered in the refrigerator. (Every time you use the starter, reserve at least 1 cup, replacing the amount you have taken out with equal amounts of flour and water. The starter will last forever, if you feed it each time you use it. There are stories of starter being passed on from generation to generation, all from an original batch). For whole wheat starter, use whole wheat flour instead of all-purpose. The method is the same.

Banana Orange Loaf

1 3/4 cups	all-purpose flour, unsifted
1/2 tsp.	baking soda
1 1/2 tsp.	baking powder
3/4 tsp.	salt (don't omit)
3/4 cup	granulated sugar
1/4 cup	vegetable oil
1 cup	mashed banana
1/2 cup	milk
2 tsp.	grated orange rind

Measure and sift all dry ingredients. Combine remaining ingredients in bowl. Stir into dry ingredients. Stir until just blended and scrape into a greased 9 x 5 inch loaf pan. Bake at 350°F (180°C) for 50 minutes.

Saffron Tea Bread

2 cups	all-purpose flour, sifted
2 tsp	baking powder
1/2 tsp	salt
1/4 tsp	soda
1/4 tsp	cinnamon
1/2 cup	shortening
3/4 cup	granulated sugar
1/8 tsp	powdered saffron
2 tsp	grated lemon peel
2	eggs
2/3 cup	water
2 tbsp	lemon juice

Pre-heat oven to 350°F (180°C). Sift together the flour, baking powder, salt, soda and cinnamon. Cream shortening, sugar, saffron, and lemon peel until fluffy. Beat in eggs, one at a time. Combine water and lemon juice and add alternately with the dry ingredients to the creamed mixture, beginning and ending with the dry ingredients.

Turn into 3 well greased 5 1/2 x 3 x 2 1/2 inch loaf pans. Bake at 350°F (180°C) for about 35 minutes. Cool in pans for10 minutes. Turn out onto wire rack for complete cooling. Spread with softened cream cheese or butter.

Best Ever Nut Loaf

3 cups	all-purpose flour, sifted
3/4 cup	granulated sugar
3 1/2 tsp	baking powder
1 1/2 tsp	salt
1	egg, beaten
1 1/2 cups	milk
2 tbsp	vegetable oil
3/4 cup	walnuts or pecans

Pre-heat oven to 350°F (180°C). Sift dry ingredients. Combine egg, milk and salad oil. Add to dry ingredients. Mix well. Stir in nuts. Bake in a greased 9 1/2 x 5 x 3 inch pan at 350°F (180°C) for 1 hour. Remove from pan; cool on rack.

Glazed Lemon Nut Bread

1/4 cup	butter
3/4 cup	granulated sugar
2	eggs
2 tsp	grated lemon peel
2 cups	all-purpose flour, sifted
2 1/2 tsp	baking powder
1 tsp	salt
3/4 cup	milk
1/2 cup	chopped walnuts or pecans
2 tsp	lemon juice
2 tbsp	granulated sugar

Cream together butter and 3/4 cup sugar until light and fluffy. Add eggs and lemon peel; beat well. Sift together flour, baking powder and salt; add to creamed mixture alternately with milk, beating until smooth after each addition. Stir in nuts. Pour into greased 8 1/2 x 4 1/2 x 2 1/2 inch loaf pan. Bake at 350°F (180°C) for 50 to 55 minutes. Let cool for 10 minutes in the pan. Spoon mixture of lemon juice and 2 tbsp of sugar over the top. Remove from pan and cool.

Frosted Ribbon Loaf

Ham Filling:

1 cup	ground cooked ham
1/3 cup	celery, finely chopped
2 tbsp	pickle relish,drained
1/2 tsp	prepared horseradish
1/4 cup	mayonnaise

Egg Filling:

4	hard cooked eggs, chopped
1/3 cup	stuffed olives, chopped
2 tbsp	green onion, finely chopped
2 tsp	prepared mustard
1/4 cup	mayonnaise
Unsliced sandwich loaf	
2 packages	cream cheese, (4 oz each), softened
1/3 cup	milk

Ham Filling: Combine ham, celery, pickle relish, horseradish, and 1/4 cup mayonnaise.

Egg Filling: Combine eggs, olives, onion, mustard, and 1/4 cup mayonnaise. Trim crusts from the loaf. Slice bread lengthwise in 3 equal layers; butter slices. Spread first slice, buttered side up, with ham filling, second slice with egg filling and end with third slice. Wrap in foil and chill. At serving time, beat cream cheese with milk until fluffy. Frost top and sides of loaf. Sprinkle generously with snipped parsley. Makes 10 slices.

Diploma Sandwiches

Unsliced whole wheat sandwich loaf
Pickle relish
Devilled Ham - 1 can, (7 1/2 oz)

Trim crusts from all side of an unsliced sandwich loaf. Slice very thinly. This is easier to do if you freeze the bread first and then partially thaw. Immediately place each slice between dampened towels to keep soft enough to roll up later on. Add a little pickle relish to canned devilled ham, and spread on slices, lightly rolling up each one as you go. Place the diplomas seam side down until time to tie in the centre with a small ribbon. Keep fresh by covering with plastic wrap and a damp towel.

Asparagus Rolls-Ups

1 can	asparagus tips, well-drained
Slices	sandwich bread to equal number of tips in the can
Butter	

Trim all the crusts off the bread. Spread with soft butter. Place one well drained and dry asparagus tip on each slice of bread. Roll up gently. Place seam side down on a platter. Cover with plastic wrap and a damp towel until ready to use.

The Evening Meal

Eating is a warm, almost sensual experience, especially during the winter months in Canada. As much as I thoroughly enjoy the summer months, with barbecues, picnicis and lighter meals; the winter months offer wonderful aromas that can make your mouth water.

The smell of a stew or hearty soup simmering on the stove, a chicken roasting in the oven or a fresh apple pie can warm you as you enter the house from the deep freeze outside.

I like dinner. It is a chance, whether during the week or on a Sunday night, for the family to dine together and to discuss the events of the day. When alone, it is time to relax, read the paper, catch up on a good book or listen to music. Whether you dine alone, with friends or family, it is basically a social event structured around a daily necessity.

Sometimes you are in a rush, either coming or going. Sometimes, you have the luxury of leisurely preparing the meal. Sometimes you have helpers (wanted and unwanted). Whatever the occasion, you will find something in this section to make your task a little easier.

With the average housewife preparing just over 1000 meals per year, you might find something different to add to your repertoire.

Cabbage and Beef Soup

2 tbsp	vegetable oil
1/2 lb.	ground beef
2	stalks celery, chopped
1	small onion, chopped
1	green pepper, chopped
1 tsp	salt
1/4 tsp	pepper
1 tsp	paprika
3 cups	beef stock
2 tsp	hot pepper sauce
2	garlic cloves, chopped
2	potatoes, cubed
2	carrots, sliced
2	parsnips, sliced
1/2 cup	kernel corn
1/2 cup	kidney beans
1 can	tomatoes, (19 fl. oz)
2 cups	red cabbage, chopped
1/4 cup	fresh parsley, chopped

In a very large saucepan or soup pot, heat oil and then brown meat until no longer pink. Add celery, onion, green pepper, garlic, salt and pepper. Cook until vegetables are tender. Drain off any fat. Add remaining ingredients, except the cabbage and the parsley. Simmer uncovered for 45 minutes to one hour. Add cabbage, simmer, covered for 45 minutes more. Add parsley and serve.

Chuck Steak Dinner

I remember when chuck steak was 44 cents a pound in 1976. Very few people at that time realized the value of a good chuck steak. I had to convince some butchers that even without marinating the steak, it was great on a BBQ. Somewhere along the way, others discovered my steak and it became much more expensive. In any event, it is still a good buy, tasty and flavourful and, most important, extremely versatile.

```
1 ................................chuck steak (sized to suit you needs)
1 can ..........................beef or onion gravy
1 package ....................dry onion soup
5 ................................medium potatoes
3 ................................medium carrots
3 ................................medium onions
```
Frozen peas
Mixed vegetables

Take the steak out of the freezer in the morning. Place in a baking dish and pour the rest of the ingredients over the meat. Season to taste with oregano, marjoram, salt, pepper, dill and celery salt and paprika. Cover tightly with foil. Bake at 350°F (180°C) for 2 hours or longer. This makes a complete meal with gravy, vegetables and meat, all in one dish. It is great with a salad and chunks of fresh bread. The clean up is easy too. During the winter months you may wish to prepare this dish in the morning, place in the oven while the meat is frozen, and set the timer to start the cooking process around 3:30. By 5:30, as you walk in the door, dinner will be ready. The aroma alone will warm your chilled bones.

Pork With Sage

```
1 ................................egg
```
Finely grated peel of one orange
```
2 tbsp. ........................fresh sage, finely chopped or 1 tsp.
                               dried sage
1/2 tsp. ......................salt
1/2 tsp .......................freshly ground pepper
1 lb. ...........................ground pork
1/4 cup ......................fine dry bread crumbs or oatmeal
1/4 tsp. ......................dry mustard
```

Whisk egg in medium bowl. Stir in orange peel, mustard and seasonings. Add meat. Sprinkle in bread crumbs. Work with hands until blended. Shape into patties. Barbecue for 6 minutes on each side.

Shrimp/Scallop/Veal Casserole

1 1/2 lb	veal cutlets
3 tbsp	butter
1 cup	onions, chopped
1 cup	fresh mushrooms, sliced
2 cups	chicken stock
3/4 cup	white wine
1 tsp	dried tarragon
1 tsp	salt
1/2 tsp	freshly ground pepper
1 lb	large shrimp, cooked
1/2 lb	large scallops, cooked
1/2 cup	whipping cream
2 tbsp each	butter and all-purpose flour, blended together

Cut veal into bite sized pieces. In a large skillet heat oil and butter. Brown veal. Using a slotted spoon transfer veal to a warm platter. Cook onions and mushrooms in the oil and butter remaining in the pan until tender. Gradually stir in stock and wine. Stir in the spices. Return the veal to the pan and cover and simmer until tender, about 25 minutes. Stir in the shrimp, scallops and simmer until heated through. Stir in cream and butter/flour mixture, stir until sauce thickens. Spoon into large shallow serving bowl. Sprinkle with parsley.

Dinners For Under $1.50 Per Serving

Use any combination of the following recipes to make a tasty but economical dinner. By adding a salad or coleslaw and a beverage, you will make the meal complete.

Onion Mushroom Burgers on Bread

4	hamburger patties (see below)

Mix one pound of lean beef with 2 large onions, chopped, and 1/2 pound of fresh mushrooms, sliced. Add 1 egg and a handful of oatmeal or bread crumbs.

Shape into patties and either broil or BBQ to required taste. Serve on a thick slice of crusty bread with a dollop of sour cream along with a nice tossed or Caesar salad.

Chicken à la King

1/4 cup	butter
1	garlic clove, minced
1/4 cup	all-purpose flour
2 cups	light cream
1 cup	chicken broth
1	egg yolk
3 cups	cooked chicken, cubed
2 tbsp	butter
2 cups	sliced mushrooms
1 tsp	oregano
1 tsp	savory
1 tsp	salt
1/4 tsp	pepper
1 tsp	lemon juice
1 cup	frozen green peas
6 cups	cooked noodles

In a saucepan, melt 1/4 cup of butter. Stir in flour and garlic and cook over medium heat for 2 minutes. Pour in the cream and the chicken stock. Whisk until smooth and thick. In a small bowl, lightly beat the egg yolk; stir in some of the hot sauce and pour egg mixture back into pan. Add chicken and simmer for about 4 minutes. In skillet, melt 2 tbsp butter and sauté mushrooms. Stir into chicken mixture. Add spices and lemon juice. Let cool. Stir in peas.

Spread 1 cup cooked egg noodles in a casserole dish. Layer with noodles and chicken mixture and repeat until all the food is used up finishing with noodles. Bake at 350°F (180°C) for 25 minutes, until casserole is heated through and it is bubbling. Serves 6.

It is better to eat your pasta than to wear it.

Stir-Fried Sausages and Veggies

1 1/2 lbs	farmers' sausages
4	large carrots
1	large onion
1	large potato
Quarter of a small turnip	
1	large garlic clove
1/2 lb	green beans
2	green onions
1/3 cup	chicken stock
1 1/2 tsp	sage
1/2 tsp	salt
1/4 tsp	each pepper and thyme
2 tsp	vegetable oil
1 1/2 tsp	Worcestershire
1 1/2 tsp	Hosin sauce
1 tbsp	oyster sauce
1/4 cup	parsley, chopped

Cut sausages into 1 inch pieces. Peel and chop carrots, onion, potatoes and turnip. Finely mince garlic. Trim beans and cut into 1 inch pieces. Trim green onions, thinly slice.

In a small bowl, combine stock, sage, salt, pepper and thyme. Set aside. Lightly grease wok with oil. Heat oil over high heat. Add sausage and fry until done on all sides. All at once, add the carrots, onion, potato, turnip and garlic. Stir fry for about 1 minute. Drizzle stock mixture over food and mix well. Cover and steam over medium heat for 5 minutes. Add beans and cover cooking for 10 minutes. Stir in Worcestershire, oyster and hosin sauces. Taste and adjust seasonings. Sprinkle with parsley and onions.

Penne Arrabiate

I first tasted this dish in a well-known Italian restaurant in Toronto. I have been hooked on it ever since. It is not overly filling, it is easy to make, and delicious to eat. I soon learned not to wear anything white when trying to eat this pasta. Invariably, I always seemed to manage to splash some on myself. Now I always wear black while eating out and tuck a large serviette into my top when eating at home.

2 tsp	olive oil
1	small onion, chopped
2	garlic cloves, minced
1 cup	canned tomatoes
1 1/2 tsp	dried basil
2 tbsp	fresh parsley, chopped
1/2 tsp	salt
1/2 tsp	pepper

Enough cooked pasta for four people. I use the penne pasta. You may wish to use another variety.

In a saucepan, heat the olive oil. Add onion and garlic and sauté until tender. Stir in tomatoes, basil, parsley, salt and pepper. Bring to a boil; reduce heat and simmer, stirring occasionally, for five minutes until slightly thickened. Pour sauce over pasta which has been cooked and drained. Great as an appetizer or main course.

Beef/Vegetable Casserole

1 can	tomatoes, (19 fl. oz)
1 tbsp	butter
3/4 cup	wild rice
1 lb	ground beef
1 tsp	salt
1/2 tsp	oregano
1/4 tsp	marjoram
1 tsp	salt
1/2 tsp	ground pepper
2 cups	cabbage, coarsely chopped
1/2 cup	green pepper
1 cup	carrots, chopped
1 tbsp	all-purpose flour
1/2 cup	plain yogurt
1 cup	Cheddar cheese, shredded

Drain tomatoes, reserving liquid. Chop tomatoes and set aside. Add enough water to liquid to make 2 cups. Pour into saucepan add butter and rice and bring to a boil. Cover tightly, reduce heat and simmer for about 30 minutes.

Meanwhile, in skillet, cook beef until browned; add salt and pepper. Remove from heat. In saucepan, cook cabbage in enough boiling water to cover, until barely tender, about 5 minutes; drain. Sprinkle with flour and toss lightly. In another saucepan, steam carrots until tender crisp.

In an 8 cup casserole, layer ingredients as follows: rice, cabbage, yogurt, beef, carrots, green pepper, chopped tomatoes and cheese. Bake uncovered at 350°F (180°C) for 20 to 30 minutes or until heated through and cheese is bubbly.

Chicken With Pears And Lime Cinnamon Sauce

1/4 cup	vegetable oil
4	chicken breasts, skinned and boned, chopped into 1 inch pieces.
1/2 lb.	snow peas
4	green onions
3	pears, sliced

Lime Cinnamon Sauce:

6 tbsp	water
1/4 cup	light soy sauce
4 tsp	granulated sugar
2 tsp	grated lime rind
1/4 cup	lime juice
1	garlic clove, minced
2 tsp	ground cinnamon

Lime Cinnamon Sauce Directions:

In bowl, combine water, soy sauce, sugar, cornstarch, lime rind, lime juice, garlic and cinnamon; set aside.

Main Dish Directions:

In large skillet or wok, heat 2 tbsp of oil, cook chicken over high heat until white, about 2 minutes. Transfer to warm plate. Add remaining oil and stir fry the snow peas for 1 to 2 minutes. Reduce heat. Add chicken, onions, pears and lime cinnamon sauce; stir cook for 1 to 2 minutes or until mixture is heated and sauce is thickened. Serve on a bed of rice or buttered noodles.

You may wish to use peaches or Japanese pears instead.

Layered Pie

This pie cuts beautifully, warm or cold, to reveal attractive layers that taste as good as they look.

1	onion, chopped
1	garlic clove, minced
1 tbsp.	butter
1	bag spinach, (10 oz), washed and stemmed

Pastry for a 9 inch pie:

8 oz.	sliced ham
8 oz.	Mozzarella cheese, sliced
1	red pepper, cut in strips
4	eggs, beaten

Sauté onion and garlic in butter until tender. Cook spinach just until wilted. Drain well and stir into onion mixture. Roll out bottom crust and fit into deep 9 inch pie plate or quiche pan. Lay ham slices on pastry. Cover with cheese, spinach and then red pepper. Reserve small amount of egg to brush on top crust. Pour remaining egg into pie. Cover with top crust. Decorate with any leftover pastry if desired. Seal edges. Brush with reserved egg. Make slits for steam to escape. Bake at 400°F (200°C) for 35 to 40 minutes or until pastry is golden. Makes 4 to 5 servings.

Salmon And Rice Cabbage Rolls

12	large cabbage leaves

Filling:

1 1/4 cups	water
1/2	long grain rice
1/2 tsp.	salt
2 tbsp.	vegetable oil
1 cup	onions, chopped
3/4 cup	celery, finely chopped
2 tbsp.	fresh parsley, chopped
1 can	salmon, (7 oz)
2 tsp.	lemon juice
1	egg, lightly beaten

Sauce:

1 can	tomato sauce, (14 fl. oz)
1 tbsp.	cider vinegar
1 tbsp.	brown sugar

Into a large pot of boiling water, plunge cabbage leaves, cook for 2 to 3 minutes or until pliable. Drain and remove heavy portion of vein from leaf.

Filling:

In a small saucepan, bring water to boil. Add rice and salt. Reduce, cover and cook for 20 minutes until liquid is absorbed.

In skillet, cook onions and celery over medium heat stirring occasionally until onions are softened. Stir into rice along with parsley, salmon, egg, and lemon juice. Mix well.

Place about 1/4 cup of filling on each leaf and roll up, tucking in ends. Place in a greased shallow baking dish large enough to have rolls in a single layer.

In a small bowl, mix together tomato sauce, vinegar and brown sugar. Pour over cabbage rolls and bake in a 350°F (180°C) oven, covered, for about 1 hour. Uncover and bake 30 minutes longer.

Old Fashioned Baked Beans

1 lb	pea beans
6 cups	water
1	large onion, chopped
1/4 lb.	bacon, diced
1/2 cup	maple syrup
1/3 cup	chili sauce
2 tbsp.	molasses
2 tsp.	Dijon mustard
2 tsp.	salt
3	apples, cored and cut into eighths
1/3 cup	firmly packed brown sugar
1/4 cup	melted butter

Wash beans and place in a large saucepan; pour water over and cover. Let stand overnight.

Bring beans to a boil and reduce heat. Simmer covered about 1 hour. Drain and reserve liquid.

In a 6 cup casserole, combine beans, onions, bacon, maple syrup, chili sauce, molasses, mustard and salt. Add enough reserved cooking liquid to cover; stir well. Cover and bake in 300°F (150°C) oven for 3 hours, stir occasionally, add more liquid if needed. Uncover and top with apple slices. Sprinkle with brown sugar and drizzle with melted butter. Serves 6 to 8.

Winter Vegetable Pasta

1/4 cup	vegetable oil
1/4 cup	butter
2	garlic cloves, minced
1 cup	leeks, chopped
2 cups	fresh mushrooms
1 1/2 cups	broccoli florets
3/4 cup	celery, chopped
3/4 cup	carrots, thinly sliced
1	zucchini, cut in 1/4 inch slices
1 tsp.	basil
1 tsp.	oregano
1/4 lb.	snow peas

1 cup	frozen green peas
1 cup	green onions, chopped
1 cup	whipping cream
1 lb.	spaghettini, cooked and drained
1 cup	Parmesan cheese, freshly grated

In a large wok, heat oil and butter over medium heat. Add garlic and leeks, cook for 2 minutes. Increase heat to medium-high and add mushrooms, broccoli, celery, carrots, zucchini and herbs, stir fry for 2 minutes. Cover and cook for 2 to 3 minutes longer. Add snow peas, green peas and onions; cook uncovered for 2 minutes, stirring constantly. Bring to a boil. Add pasta and Parmesan, toss to combine.

Clam/Sole Soup

3	potatoes, unpeeled, halved and sliced
1 can	clams
2	stalks celery, sliced
2 cups	chicken stock or two cups tomato juice
1 lb.	fresh or frozen fish
1 cup	frozen green peas

Salt and freshly ground pepper

Drain clams, reserve liquid and set aside. In large skillet, combine potatoes, celery, stock or juice and liquid from clams. Bring to a boil, reduce heat and simmer for 15 to 18 minutes. Cut fish into bite-sized pieces, add to mixture in pan along with clams and peas. Simmer for 10 to 15 minutes. Season with salt and pepper.

Gazpacho Soup

A dear friend of mine calls this soup his "liquid salad". We discovered a great version of Gazpacho at Toronto's York Street Movenpick Restaurant. I was challenged to make one as tasty. Fortunately for me, and unbeknownst to my friend, I took up the challenge as I had already tried out this terrific version from **RECIPES ONLY**.

My attempt was deemed a success, thanks, in part, to this wonderful recipe. If you like a soup which is flavourful, spicy, crunchy and delicious, you will enjoy this creation.

4	medium fresh tomatoes, chopped or (19 oz can of stewed tomatoes)
1	medium onion, chopped
1	medium cucumber, chopped
1	small sweet pepper, chopped
1	small hot pepper, finely chopped
1	garlic clove, crushed
4 tbsp	parsley, finely chopped
3 cups	water
2 tbsp	olive oil
2 tbsp	lemon juice
2 tsp	salt
1/2 tsp	pepper
1/2 cup	croutons
1/2 cup	chopped green olives

In a food processor, process all ingredients except croutons and olives until the vegetables turn to liquid, or if you prefer a crunchy Gazpacho, chop in the blender to desired texture. Place in a large bowl. Chill thoroughly before serving. Garnish with a lemon slice or with chopped cilantro or parsley. Serve croutons and olives in separate dishes.

(Recipe courtesy of Recipes Only, September/October, 1987, Page 218 Issue 23).

Hearty Super Fritatta

1/2 lb.	bacon, cut into strips
1	onion, thinly sliced
1	garlic clove, minced
1	small sweet pepper, cored, seeded and chopped
1	small red pepper, cored, seeded and chopped
1	tomato, chopped
2	small zucchini, finely diced
5	new potatoes, cooked and cubed
6	eggs
1 tsp.	salt
1/4 tsp.	freshly ground pepper
1/4 cup	grated Cheddar cheese
2 tbsp.	grated Parmesan cheese

In a large deep skillet, cook bacon until almost crisp. Remove with slotted spoon and drain on a paper towel. Set aside. Save 2 tbsp. of drippings and add onion and garlic and cook. Cook for 3 to 4 minutes. Stir in green pepper, tomato, zucchini. Cook, stirring occasionally, for 4 to 5 minutes. Stir in potatoes and bacon, cook, stirring lightly, for 2 minutes longer.

Meanwhile, in a large bowl, whisk together eggs, salt and pepper. Pour over vegetables and cook for 3 minutes until eggs begin to set. Sprinkle Cheddar cheese over eggs. Increase heat and continue cooking until eggs are cooked. Sprinkle with Parmesan cheese before serving. Makes 6 servings.

Savory Lamb Chops

```
4 .....................................lamb shoulder chops
1 tbsp ...........................oil
1 ....................................garlic clove, crushed
1 ....................................bay leaf
1 ....................................medium onion, sliced
1 can ...........................tomatoes, (14 fl. oz)
1/4 cup ......................mushrooms, sliced
6 ....................................black olives, pitted and sliced
Salt and pepper
```

Season and brown lamb chops on both sides in oil with the garlic. Drain off any excess fat. Add other ingredients, except the olives, and simmer uncovered for 20 to 30 minutes. Remove bay leaf and add the olives. Serve immediately.

Stir Fry Lamb and Vegetables

```
1 lb.............................ground lamb
2 tbsp. ........................corn oil
1 ....................................onion, sliced
1/4 cup ......................dry white wine
1 lb.............................green beans
1/2 cup ......................chicken stock
1 tbsp. ........................soy sauce
2 ....................................firm tomatoes
1 ....................................green pepper
1 tbsp .........................cornstarch
1 tbsp .........................water
```

Slice meat into small strips. Heat oil in wok and add meat. Stir frequently. Stir in the onion and then add the wine and the beans along with the soy sauce and chicken stock. Cover pan and reduce heat. Simmer for 5 minutes. Add chopped tomatoes and green pepper. Cook for 3 more minutes. Make a paste with cornstarch and water. Add to mixture and cook until thickened.

Poached Chicken Breasts with Berries

4 ....chicken breasts, skinned and boned
1 1/2 cups ....water
1/2 cup ....white wine
1/2 cup ....puréed strawberries
2 tbsp. ....granulated sugar

Poach chicken breasts, in a combination of water and wine. You may wish to increase the amount of wine to enhance taste. You would then reduce the amount of water accordingly. Bring the liquid to a boil and cook for about 10 minutes. Remove chicken from pan and continue to boil the liquid until reduced by about one quarter. Add 1/2 cup of strawberry purée and continue cooking. Strain liquid and reduce once more by about one quarter. Place chicken on serving platter and pour sauce over. You may wish to garnish the meat with slices of berries.

Lamb with Chutney

1 ....egg
3 tbsp. ....mango chutney
1 tsp. ....ground cumin
1/2 tsp. ....salt
1/2 tsp. ....ground coriander
1/2 cup ....bread crumbs
1 lb..............................ground lamb

Whisk egg in a large bowl. Add chutney and seasonings. Stir until blended. Add meat and work with hands. Shape into patties. Barbecue 5 minutes per side.

Beef with Horseradish

```
1 ................................egg
1/4 cup ......................sour cream
1 tbsp .........................horseradish
1 tsp ...........................Dijon mustard
1/2 tsp .......................thyme
1/4 tsp .......................salt
Freshly ground pepper
1/2 cup ......................dry bread crumbs
1 lb.............................ground beef
```

Whisk egg in a bowl. Stir in sour cream, horseradish, mustard and seasonings. Add bread crumbs and blend. Add meat and work together. Shape into patties. Barbecue 5 minutes per side.

Shrimps/Scallops/Kiwi Fruit

```
1 3/4 cups ...................fine dry bread crumbs
1 tsp ...........................salt
1 dash .........................pepper
1/4 tsp .......................basil
1/4 tsp .......................garlic powder
2 ................................eggs
2 tsp ...........................water
2 tbsp .........................lime juice
1 lb.............................large sea scallops
1 lb.............................shrimp, cooked, cleaned and
                                chopped into bite-sized pieces
1/2 cup ......................butter
4 ................................kiwis, peeled and sliced 1/4 inch thick
Chopped parsley
Hot cooked wild rice
```

Mix together the bread crumbs and spices in a flat dish. Beat together eggs, water and lime juice in another flat dish. Roll the fish, first in the bread crumbs and then in the egg/water mixture. Finally, roll in the crumbs.Melt the butter in a wok. Add shrimp and scallops and cook until batter is golden on all sides. Lift out of the wok with a slotted spoon and place on a warm platter covered with a paper towel. Keep warm. Treat the kiwi fruit in the same manner as the fish. Add more butter if necessary and cook the kiwi until the batter is golden. Remove to same platter as the fish.

Daddy making homemade soup.

Using a fresh platter, decorated with parsley, spread the fruit and fish on a bed of wild rice.

Goulash Soup

My father liked to have fun in the kitchen. He used to wear a pair of old grey pants which we called "Daddy's Soup Pants". The reason was obvious: whenever Daddy made a big batch of soup with everything but the kitchen sink included, he always wore his special grey pants. One day, Mum tried to donate them to a greater cause and lo and behold, Daddy must have rescued them, because the next time he made soup, there they were! Mum never did get rid of them. I think they eventually disintegrated in the washing machine. Nonetheless, Daddy still makes great soup, with or without his pants. (Not to be taken literally).

1/4 cup	shortening
2 lb	lean stewing beef, cut into 1 inch cubes
2 1/2 cups	onions, sliced
3 tbsp	caraway seed
2 tbsp	paprika
2 tbsp	garlic powder
1 can	tomatoes, (28 fl.oz), undrained
2 cups	green pepper, chopped
2 tsp	basil
1/2 cup	beer, if desired
2 cups	carrots, chopped
4 cups	potatoes, chopped
10 cups	beef stock
2 tsp	majoram
Pepper	
1/2 lb	egg noodles, cooked

In a large soup pot, melt shortening; brown beef and onions. Remove from heat and stir in caraway seeds, paprika, garlic powder and salt. Cover very tightly and cook meat in its own juice over low heat for about 20 minutes. Stir in tomatoes, green pepper, basil and 1/2 cup beer, if using. Cover and cook over medium heat for about 1 more hour. (Just imagine all the flavours blending together. Besides, the aroma in the house will be terrific).

Add the potatoes and carrots along with the stock. Cover and simmer until the vegetables are tender and the meat is cooked. This should take about 30 minutes. Taste and season with more pepper and paprika if necessary. Stir in majoram. Heat for 3 to 4 minutes longer. This is best made the day before and then re-heated. Serve with hot cooked egg noodles.

Lucy Gray's Great Cabbage Pie

Crust:

3/4 cup	shredded Mozzarella or Swiss Cheese
1 cup	whole wheat flour
1 cup	rolled oats
1/4 cup	wheat germ
1/4 cup	grated Parmesan cheese
1/2 cup	butter

Filling:

2 tbsp	butter
4 cups	shredded cabbage
1	onion, chopped
1	small red pepper, chopped
Parsley	

Custard:

4	eggs
1 cup	sour cream
1/2 cup	shredded Mozzarella or Swiss cheese
2 tbsp	Parmesan cheese
1/2 tsp	dried basil
1/2 tsp	dried oregano

Crust: In a medium bowl, mix together cheese, flour, oats, wheat germ and Parmesan. With fingers blend in butter until mixture is crumbly. Remove one cup and set aside. Press the remaining mixture into a 9 inch springform pan, evenly across the bottom and part way up the sides. Set aside.

Filling: In skillet, melt butter; sauté cabbage, onion and pepper just until limp, about 5 minutes. Spoon into crust.

Custard: Beat eggs, blend in the rest of the ingredients. Pour over filling and sprinkle the remaining 1 cup of the crust mixture over the top. Bake at 375°F (190°C) until centre is set. Let cool 20 minutes. Cut into wedges.

Skillet Stew from the Sea

1 lb	cod, partially thawed to make cutting easier
1/8 tsp	marjoram
1/8 tsp	oregano
2 tbsp	olive oil
1	garlic clove, minced
1	bay leaf, crushed
1/2 cup	onion, coarsely chopped
1 can	tomatoes, (14 fl. oz)
1	potato, diced
1	cucumber, unpeeled and sliced

Cut fish into cubes; sprinkle with marjoram and oregano. Set aside. Heat olive oil in a large, covered skillet. Add bay leaf, garlic and onion, sauté lightly for about 2 1/2 minutes. Add vegetables and a little salt if desired. Cover and let simmer for about 7 minutes. Add the fish and cover and simmer for another 15 to 20 minutes. You may wish to add half a can of tomato paste if you prefer a thicker base.

Randy's Cheese/Fish Casserole

l-1/2 lb	fish (I use perch)
4 cups	chicken stock
1	onion
1	garlic clove, crushed
3	cloves
Salt and pepper	
2 tbsp	butter
1 1/4 cups	white sauce
2	eggs
1/2 cup	grated Cheddar cheese
1 1/4 cups	milk

Cut fish into one inch pieces. Put fish into an electric frying pan and cover with stock. Peel and thinly slice onion, add to fish together with cloves and crushed garlic. Bring mixture slowly to a boil and season with salt and pepper. Simmer for about 10 minutes and remove fish from liquid. Measure out 1 1/2 cups of stock. Strain and set aside for use in the making of the white sauce.

White Sauce:

Melt 3 1/4 tsp of butter in a large saucepan. Add 3 1/4 tsp flour. Stir flour completely into butter. Gradually add strained stock, about 1 cup. Heat and continue stirring over medium heat until sauce begins to thicken. Add more stock if necessary. Flake fish into greased casserole dish, removing any bones. Pour white sauce over fish and coat thoroughly. Beat eggs, salt and pepper. Add grated cheese and milk. Pour mixture over fish. Bake at 325°F (160°C) for 45 minutes or until custard is set. Serve with rice.

Chicken/Snow Peas/Cherry Tomato Stir-fry

1 1/2 lbs	boneless, skinless chicken breast
1 tbsp	white wine
1 tbsp	soy sauce
1 tbsp	cornstarch
5 tbsp	cooking oil
2	garlic cloves, minced
1 tbsp	grated fresh gingerroot

2 ....green onions, chopped
1/2 lb..........................snow peas
2 cups ....cherry tomatoes
Sauce:
1/2 cup ....chicken stock
2 tbsp ....soy sauce
2 tsp............................cornstarch
1 tsp............................Chinese sesame oil

Cut chicken into 1 1/2 inch pieces. Place in a bowl. Add soy sauce, white wine and cornstarch. Mix well and let marinade for about 20 minutes. If you so desire, you may wish to do this the night before. Cover tightly with plastic wrap and refrigerate overnight and all day.

Have ready all the other ingredients. Make the sauce by combining all the ingredients. In a wok, heat 3 tbsp oil. Add the chicken and stir-fry until the chicken is no longer pink. Add garlic, grated gingerroot and green onions. Add remaining oil. Stir-fry 1 minute until fragrant. Add snow peas and stir-fry one more minute. Add cherry tomatoes and stir-fry, another minute. Stir sauce mixture (cornstarch tends to sink to the bottom) and pour over contents in wok. Heat until the sauce comes to a boil and thickens. Taste and season accordingly.

Zucchini Strata

4 slices	buttered bread
1/4 cup	fresh parsley
8 slices	bacon
6	green onions, sliced
4	zucchini, sliced and unpeeled
1/2 tsp	salt
Freshly ground pepper	
1 cup	sour cream
2	eggs, separated
1/2 tsp	salt
Pepper and nutmeg	
1 1/4 cups	grated Cheddar cheese

In a blender, process bread slices into crumbs. Add parsley and process until chopped. Set aside. Cook bacon until crisp. Remove with slotted spoon and drain on paper towels. Set crumbs aside. In bacon drippings, sauté onions until soft. Remove with slotted spoon onto paper towel. Mix with bacon. Lightly sauté zucchini 2 to 3 minutes. Sprinkle with 1/2 tsp salt and pepper to taste. Remove from heat. Blend sour cream with egg yolks, 1/4 tsp salt and a little pepper and nutmeg. Beat egg whites until stiff but not dry; fold into sour cream sauce. Fold in 1 cup of cheese. In a 6 cup casserole, layer half the zucchini, then half the bacon and onions, half the sour cream sauce. Layer again. Top with remaining cheese, then crumbs and parsley. Refrigerate until dinner time. Bake at 350°F (180°C) for 25 minutes.

Kahlua Slim Chicken

4	single chicken breasts, boned and skinned
1/3 cup	Kahlua
1 1/2 tbsp	wine vinegar
1 tsp	prepared mustard
1/2 tsp	paprika
1/4 tsp	celery salt
1 tsp	cornstarch

Lightly pound chicken breasts to flatten slightly. Cut each breast lengthwise into 3 strips. Ripple loosely on 8 to 10 inch meat skewers. Stir Kahlua with all remaining ingredients. Simmer, stirring, until thickened and smooth. Brush over both sides of chicken. Broil about 7 inches from heat for 10 minutes, brushing once with marinade. Turn skewer, brush again and continue broiling just until chicken is done, 5 to 10 minutes longer. Spoon any leftover marinade over the chicken when serving.

(Recipe courtesy of Kahlua).

Kahlua Neptune Sole

1/4 cup	Kahlua
1 tbsp	butter
1 tbsp	lemon juice
1 tsp	prepared mustard
4	sole fillets
Celery salt	
Dried dill	
White pepper	
Lemon wedges	
1/4 cup	green onion, finely chopped
1 tbsp	parsley, finely chopped
4 slices	firm ripe tomato
2 slices	processed Swiss cheese

Heat Kahlua with butter, lemon juice and mustard. Brush over sides of each fillet. Sprinkle each lightly with celery salt, dill and pepper. Add onion and parsley to one half of each slice, fold other end over to enclose seasonings. Top each with a tomato slice and arrange in small shallow oiled baking pan. Brush with remaining Kahlua mixture. Bake in moderately hot oven 400°F (200°C) until fish is done, about 10 minutes. Remove and place a half slice cheese on each portion (heat will melt the cheese). Garnish with lemon wedge.

(Recipe courtesy of Kahlua).

Texas Coleslaw

1	medium cabbage, shredded
1	medium green pepper, chopped
1	large onion, finely chopped
1	carrot, grated
1/2 cup	vegetable oil
1/2 cup	vinegar
1/2 cup	granulated sugar
1 tsp.	salt
1/2 tsp.	dry mustard
2 tbsp.	parsley, freshly chopped
1/4 tsp.	pepper

The day before serving, put vegetables in mixing bowl, and toss lightly.

In another bowl, combine remaining ingredients and beat until smooth and blended. Pour dressing over vegetables. Toss and refrigerate overnight. Serve the next day.

Chicken and Cheddar Casserole

5 cups	bread, cubed
1 1/2 cups	cooked chicken
1 pkg.	frozen, chopped broccoli, thawed and drained
2 cups	shredded Cheddar cheese
6	eggs
3 cups	milk
1	small onion, finely chopped
1 tsp.	dry mustard

Butter a 6 cup, deep, straight sided baking dish. Layer 1/3 of each of the bread, chicken, broccoli and cheese in the baking dish; repeat to make two more layers. Beat eggs with milk, onion, salt and mustard until blended. Pour egg mixture over strata. Cover and refrigerate at least three hours or overnight. Bake uncovered in 350°F (180°C) oven for 1 1/4 hours or until puffy and golden. Serves 6 to 8. You may substitute ham, turkey, tuna, salmon, crab and bacon. You could also substitute other vegetables such as mushrooms, asparagus or cauliflower.

Chicken Espangol

2 1/2 - 3 lbs.	broiler or fryer chicken, cut up
3 tbsp	butter
3 cups	fresh mushrooms, sliced
1 cup	onion, chopped
1	garlic clove, crushed
2 tsp.	chicken bouillon mix
1 tsp.	salt
1 tsp.	paprika
3/4 tsp.	ground ginger
1/2 tsp.	chili powder
1 can	tomatoes, (19 fl. oz)
1/2 cup	water
1/3 cup	all-purpose flour
1 1/4 cups	milk

In frying pan, brown chicken in butter; remove. Sauté mushrooms, onion, garlic. Blend in bouillon mix, salt, spices, tomatoes and water. Return chicken to pan, simmer, covered, for 40 minutes or until tender. Remove chicken and keep warm. Combine flour and milk, stir into pan juices. Cook and stir until mixture thickens. Pour over chicken. Serve with noodles. Serves 4 to 5.

Celery Ham Casserole

4 cups	celery, chopped
2 cups	potatoes, diced
3 tbsp.	butter
3 tbsp.	all-purpose flour
1 1/2 cups	milk
1/2 tsp.	dried leaf basil
1/8 tsp.	dry mustard
1 tsp.	salt
1/4 tsp.	pepper
2 cups	slivered cooked ham
1/2 cup	slivered toasted almonds

Heat oven to 375°F (190°C). Butter a shallow baking dish (9 x 9 inches). Combine celery and potatoes in a saucepan. Add a little boiling water, cover and cook until tender crisp. Drain immediately. Melt butter in saucepan. Sprinkle in flour and let bubble together. Remove from heat and add milk all at once. Stir to blend. Return to moderate heat, cook and stir until thickened and smooth. Boil 1 minute, stirring. Remove from heat and stir in basil, dry mustard, salt, pepper, ham and cooked vegetables. Pour into prepared pan. Sprinkle with almonds. Bake 15 to 20 minutes or until bubbling. Serve immediately. Serves 4.

Baked Ocean Perch

1 lb.	frozen ocean perch fillets
1/8 cup	butter, melted

Brush one side of fish with butter. Bake at 350°F (180°C) for about 15 minutes. Turn fish over and brush with remaining butter. Bake an additional 10 minutes or until fish is cooked to your taste preference. Serve with steamed potatoes and vegetables of your choice. Choose colourful ones to complement your plate.

Italian Noodle Soup

2 tbsp.	olive oil
2 tbsp.	butter
1	large onion, chopped
1	garlic clove, minced
1/2 cup	celery, chopped
1/2 cup	carrots, chopped
1/2 cup	green pepper, chopped
2 tbsp.	parsley, chopped
1 tsp.	dried basil
Salt and pepper	
2 cups	Italian plum tomatoes
2 tbsp.	tomato paste
1 can	beef broth
3 cups	water
1/2 cup	macaroni or other small pasta
1 cup	canned red kidney beans
2 cups	shredded cabbage

In a large heavy saucepan, heat oil and butter. Add onion, garlic, celery, carrots and green pepper, cook a few minutes until softened without browning. Add parsley, basil and a little salt and pepper. Stir in tomatoes, tomato paste, broth and water. Bring to a boil, reduce heat, cover and simmer for about 20 minutes. Add macaroni, cover and cook until nearly tender. Add beans and cabbage. Cover and simmer about 30 minutes. At this stage, the soup will be very thick and rich; dilute with water to desired consistency. Taste and adjust seasoning. Makes 8 to 10 servings.

Vegetable Stuffed Pork Chops

1/4 cup	butter
1 cup	onions, finely chopped
1 cup	mushrooms, finely chopped
2 cups	soft bread crumbs
1 cup	carrots, finely grated
1/2 cup	parsley, chopped
1	egg, lightly beaten
1 1/2 tsp.	lemon juice
2 tsp.	salt
1/4 tsp.	pepper
1/8 tsp.	nutmeg
6	loin pork chops (1 1/2 inches thick)
1	garlic clove, cut in half
1 tsp.	salt
1/4 tsp.	thyme
1/4 tsp.	sage
Cooking oil	
1/4 cup	water

Cut pocket in the side of chops to make room for stuffing. Heat oven to 450°F (230°C). Have ready a large shallow pan about 13 x 9 1/2 x 2 inches. Heat butter in heavy skillet. Add onions and cook gently until transparent. Add mushrooms and continue cooking gently 1 minute. Add half of the crumbs, cook and stir until crumbs are golden.

Combine remaining crumbs, carrots, parsley, egg, lemon juice, 2 tsp salt, pepper and nutmeg in a bowl. Add onion-mushroom mixture and toss lightly together.

Trim excess fat from chops. Rub on both sides with cut sides of garlic clove. Combine 1 tsp salt, thyme and sage and rub a little of this mixture on each chop. Stuff pockets of chops with prepared stuffing. Do not pack. Fasten with toothpicks. Sprinkle any leftover bread-vegetable mixture in bottom of baking pan. Lay stuffed chops on top of this mixture in a single layer. Brush with oil. Bake uncovered 30 minutes at 450°F (230°C) or until lightly browned. Reduce oven heat to 350°F (180°C). Add 1/4 cup of water and cover tightly, using aluminum foil. Cook about 1 hour or until tender. Serves 6.

Mum's Potato Kugel

2 ....eggs, beaten
1/2 tsp ....baking powder
1 tsp............................salt
1/8 tsp ....pepper
1/2 cup ....milk
3 cups ....grated potatoes
1/2 ....medium onion, grated
1 tbsp ....margarine
Paprika to sprinkle on top
Grated Cheddar Cheese, (about 1/2 cup)

Mix eggs, baking powder, seasonings, milk, potatoes, onions. Layer or mix in cheese. Dot with margarine and sprinkle with paprika. Bake at 350°F (180°C) for 1 hour and 15 minutes or until done. If you are in a hurry, bake the night before and then re-heat. Serves 6 people.

Noodle Corned Beef Supper

2 pouches	vacuum packed corned beef, cut in strips
12 oz.	broad or medium noodles
2 tbsp	butter
1/4 cup	green pepper, chopped
1/4 cup	onion, chopped
2	eggs
1/4 cup	milk

Salt and pepper
Parmesan cheese

Cook noodles in salted boiling water until tender. Meanwhile in frying pan, melt butter, sauté green pepper and onion, cook 3 minutes. Add sliced corned beef and stir to mix. Keep warm.

Beat eggs, milk, salt and pepper. Add egg and meat mixtures to hot, well-drained noodles. Toss well. Season with salt and pepper. Sprinkle generously with freshly grated Parmesan cheese. Serve immediately. Serves 4.

Mandarin Salad

1 can	mandarin orange segments
1	crisp, tart apple
1 cup	seedless grapes
1/4 cup	yogurt
2 tsp	liquid honey

Drain oranges and place in a bowl. Core apple, but do not peel, cut into 1 inch pieces and combine with oranges. Add grapes. Combine yogurt and honey; pour over fruit and toss gently. Chill until ready to serve.

Strawberry Shortcake

4 cups	all-purpose flour
4 tbsp.	baking powder
1 tsp.	soda
1 cup	granulated sugar
1 tsp.	salt

1 cup .... shortening
2 cups .... sour milk
1 quart .... strawberries

Mix the dry ingredients and the shortening until they resemble coarse meal. Add the milk and just mix enough to make sure dry part is moistened. Spread the dough out in a greased 13 x 9 x 2 inch cake pan. Sprinkle sugar over the top of the batter. Bake at 400°F (200°C) for about 20 minutes. Smother cake with berries. Serve warm.

Apple Crisp

4 cups .... sliced, tart apples (about 4 medium)
2/3 cup .... packed brown sugar
1/2 cup .... all-purpose flour
1/2 cup .... rolled oats
3/4 tsp. .... ground cinnamon
3/4 tsp. .... ground nutmeg
1/3 cup .... butter, softened

Heat oven to 375°F (190°C). Arrange apples in a greased 8 x 8 x 2 inch square pan. Mix remaining ingredients; sprinkle over apples. Bake until topping is golden brown and apples are tender, about 30 minutes. Serve warm with ice cream. Serves 6.

Raspberry Snow

1 envelope	unflavoured gelatin
2 cups	milk
1/4 cup	granulated sugar
1/2 cup	puréed fresh or frozen raspberries
2 tbsp.	lemon juice
1 tsp.	lemon rind
1 tsp.	grated orange rind
2	egg whites, stiffly beaten

Sprinkle gelatin over milk. Let soften. Add sugar, place over medium heat, stir until gelatin and sugar are dissolved. Cool. Add puréed fruit, lemon juice and rind. Chill in refrigerator until slightly jellied. Fold stiffly beaten egg whites into fruit mixture and chill until set. Garnish with extra rind. Makes 6 servings.

Applesauce Cake

2 1/2 cups	all-purpose flour
2 cups	granulated sugar
1 1/2 tsp.	baking soda
1 1/2 tsp.	salt
1/4 tsp.	baking powder
3/4 tsp.	ground cinnamon
1/2 tsp.	ground cloves
1/2 tsp.	ground allspice
1 1/2 cups	applesauce
1/2 cup	water
1/2 cup	shortening
2	eggs
1 cup	raisins
1/2 cup	chopped walnuts

Heat oven to 350°F (180°C). Grease and flour a 13 x 9 x 2 inch oblong pan. Beat all ingredients in a large mixer bowl on low speed. Scrape bowl constantly. Beat for 30 seconds. Beat on high speed, scraping bowl occasionally, for 3 minutes. Pour into pan. Bake until wooden pick inserted in centre comes out clean, for 60 to 65 minutes. Cool.

Rush Hour Dinners

Getting dinner on the table quickly is an art. It is a well accepted fact that the time period between 4 and 6 in the evening is the worst time of day, especially for Mums at home with small children. Working parents also face the hassle of having to prepare dinner the minute they walk in the door. This is not an easy task. The longest preparation time for the following dishes is 20 minutes. Other dishes take just a matter of minutes. In truth, it does help if you have some of the ingredients prepared ahead of time. You may wish to do this the night before, or have a youngster, aged 11 or older, do some of it for you after school. If you have children old enough to cook, say 14 or older, assign them one night per week to make their favourite dish. They will get a chance to improve their culinary skills, and you will be able to enjoy a night away from the kitchen.

Stir-Fried Beef with Broccoli and Red Pepper

1 lb	blade or sirloin steak
2	garlic cloves, minced
2 tbsp	soy sauce
1 bunch	broccoli
1	sweet red pepper, sliced
1/4 cup	vegetable oil

Cut beef into long strips, 2 inches wide. Then cut into 1/2 strips lengthwise. Place in a small bowl and stir in garlic and soy sauce. Cover and refrigerate for at least 2 hours, stirring occasionally. Cut broccoli tops into small florets. Peel larger stem and cut into 1 inch sticks. Set wok over high heat and add half the oil and heat for 20 seconds. Stir in beef mixture, all at once. Stir-fry for 3 to 4 minutes or until the colour of the meat has changed. Push to one side. Heat remaining oil, add broccoli and red pepper and stir-fry for 2 minutes. Add 2 tbsp. of water and cover and cook over low heat for about 5 minutes. Uncover, and mix beef in with the rest of the ingredients. Broccoli should be tender crisp. Serve on rice.

Braised Leeks with Ocean Perch

3	medium leeks
1/3 cup	butter
1 1/4 lbs	ocean perch fillets, partially thawed
1/2 tsp	marjoram
1/4 tsp	oregano
1 tbsp	parsley, chopped

Trim roots and green parts off leeks. Cut in half lengthwise. Wash and slice thinly. In a large heavy skillet, melt butter and stir in leeks until coated with butter. Cover pan and cook over very low heat for 5 minutes. Make sure the leeks do not stick to the pan. Add a few drops of water if necessary. Place fish fillets on top of the leeks and sprinkle with majoram and oregano. Cover tightly and increase temperature slightly. Cook until fish flakes easily with a fork, about 10 to 15 minutes. Serve on hot plates, sprinkle with freshly chopped parsley.

Minute Minestrone

2 tbsp	butter
1	onion, chopped
1	garlic clove, finely chopped
1/2 lb	pork sausage, cut into 1 inch pieces
2 cups	chicken stock
2 cups	shredded cabbage
1 can	red kidney beans, (19 fl. oz)
4	tomatoes, chopped
1	carrot, diced
1 tsp	salt
1/4 tsp	pepper
1 1/2 cups	elbow macaroni

In a large saucepan, heat butter and sauté onion and garlic until tender but not brown. Add sausage and cook, stirring gently, until lightly browned. Add stock, cabbage, kidney beans, tomatoes, carrot and seasonings; bring to a boil. Reduce heat slightly and cook until vegetables are tender, about 10 minutes. For thicker soup cook 10 minutes longer. Meanwhile, cook macaroni in boiling, salted water. Drain and stir into soup. Taste and adjust seasonings.

Sweet and Sour Pork

1 lb	boneless pork shoulder
2 tbsp	soy sauce
1	garlic clove, minced
2 tbsp	vegetable oil
Salt and pepper	
1	green pepper, cut into 1 inch squares
1	small carrot, very thinly sliced
3/4 cup	granulated sugar
2 tbsp	cornstarch
1 cup	pineapple juice, reserved from can
1/3 cup	vinegar
3 tbsp	tomato paste
1 cup	pineapple chunks, canned
1 cup	kiwi fruit

Cut pork into 1 inch cubes. Marinate in soy sauce while preparing vegetables. In a large frying pan, heat oil and sauté garlic. Brown pork over medium high heat, then reduce heat and cook about 5 minutes longer or until pork is cooked through. Sprinkle lightly with salt and pepper. Add green pepper and carrot; stir-fry until nearly tender.

In a small bowl, mix together sugar and cornstarch. Stir in pineapple juice, vinegar, tomato paste and 1/4 tsp salt. Drain any excess fat from frying pan. Pour sauce over meat in pan; bring to a boil, stir until smooth and thick. Add the pineapple and kiwi fruit, simmer for about 1 minute.

Cheese Pie with Hamburger Crust

Crust:

1	egg
1/2 cup	milk
3 slices	bread, cubed

In a large mixing bowl, beat eggs slightly. Add milk and bread. Toss lightly. Then let it stand for a few minutes until most of the liquid is absorbed.

1/2 lb	ground beef
1 tsp	Worcestershire sauce
1 tsp	salt
1/4 tsp	thyme
1/4 tsp	dried parsley
1 1/4 cups	green onions, sliced

Add beef to bread mixture along with Worcestershire sauce, salt, thyme, parsley and half the onions. Mix until well combined. Spoon into a 9 inch pie plate and spread to line bottom and sides of plate. Sprinkle remaining green onions over crust.

Filling:

3	eggs
1/2 tsp	salt
Dash of pepper	
1 cup	grated Cheddar cheese
1/3 cup	milk
Paprika	

Beat eggs until foamy. Stir in cheese and seasonings (except paprika) and milk. Pour over green onions in meat crust. Sprinkle lightly with paprika. Centre will be soft, but set when done. Bake at 350°F (180°C) for 30 to 40 minutes.

Noodle Onion Pie

Cheese Pie Shell:

1 cup	grated Cheddar cheese
3/4 cup	all-purpose flour
1/2 tsp	salt
1/4 tsp	dry mustard
1/4 cup	melted butter

Combine all of the above ingredients in a bowl. Mix with a fork until smooth. Knead about 1 minute to soften, then, without rolling, press firmly on the bottom and sides of 9 inch pie plate and flute the edge.

Filling:

1 1/4 cups	noodles
1 1/2 cups	onion, thinly sliced
2 tbsp	butter
2	eggs
1 cup	milk
1 tsp	salt
1/4 tsp	pepper
1 cup	grated Cheddar Cheese

Cook and drain noodles. Sauté onion in butter in frying pan until tender but not brown. Remove from heat add noodles and toss lightly. Put in unbaked cheese pie shell. Beat eggs slightly and slowly stir in milk. Add salt, pepper and cheese. Pour over noodles and bake in 325°F (160°C) oven for 50 to 60 minutes or until knife inserted in the centre of the pie comes out clean. Cool slightly before cutting.

Mexican Style Chili

```
1 package .................... dry kidney beans, (14 oz)
1/4 lb ........................ salt pork, diced
3 ................................ garlic cloves, minced
2 ................................ large onions, chopped
1 lb............................ lean beef, diced
1 lb............................ lean pork, diced,
1 can .......................... tomato sauce, (14 fl. oz)
3 tbsp ........................ chili powder
2 tsp........................... salt
1/4 tsp ....................... pepper
1/2 tsp ....................... dry oregano
Pinch cumin
Tomato juice (up to 19 fl. oz)
```

Wash and look over beans. Soak in 6 cups of cold water overnight. Drain.

Cook salt pork in a large skillet or Dutch oven until very crisp. Add garlic and onions and cook and stir until limp. Add beef and pork and cook, stirring gently until lightly browned. Stir in all remaining ingredients except the tomato juice. Cover tightly and simmer 1 1/2 hours or until meat and beans are tender. If the pan appears to be getting dry (chili should be moist but not wet when cooking is finished) add tomato juice a little at a time. Taste and adjust seasoning.

Carrot Cheddar Casserole

1 lb.	carrots, cooked and mashed (about 2 cups)
1 1/2 cups	milk
1 cup	grated Cheddar cheese
1 cup	cracker crumbs
2 tbsp	melted butter
1 tsp	salt
2	eggs

Combine all ingredients. Pour into a greased casserole dish and bake at 350°F (180°C) for 30 minutes.

Mushroom Potato Casserole

6	medium potatoes
2	eggs, beaten
1/4 cup	butter
1/4 cup	milk

Peel potatoes. Steam until soft but still firm. Beat with mixer. Add remaining ingredients. Beat until fluffy.

1	large onion, sliced
1/4 cup	butter
3/4 lb	mushrooms, sliced
Salt	
Pepper	
2 tbsp	parsley, chopped

Sauté onion for 5 minutes. Add mushrooms, salt and pepper. Cook for 5 minutes. Grease a large casserole and line with potatoes. Cover with mushroom mixture. Add remaining potatoes. Bake at 400°F (200°C) for 15 to 20 minutes in a covered dish. You may wish to sprinkle the casserole with 1 1/2 cups of grated Cheddar cheese. Garnish with parsley.

A Mixed Bag

Here are recipes which are hard to put into a section by themselves, as they are difficult to categorize. Therefore, I shall be honest with you. I did not know where to put them, so here they are. They have all been tested and, believe me, they are delicious.

Ham Stacks

2 packages	sliced ham
1 package	cream cheese, (8 oz), softened
2 tbsp	hot horseradish
2 tbsp	Dijon mustard

Dry the pieces of ham between paper towel. Cream all other ingredients and spread a small portion on the first slice of ham. Add additional slices of ham, spreading each one with cream mixture. Wrap in foil and refrigerate. Before serving, slice ham stack into bite-sized pieces. Serve with a toothpick. This recipe is easy to double.

Ham and Cheese Quiches

Pastry for 2 crust 9 inch pie.

1 1/2 cups	grated Swiss cheese
2	eggs, beaten
3/4 cup	light cream
2 tbsp	onion, finely chopped
1 can	devilled ham, (4 1/2 oz)
1 tsp	Dijon mustard
1/2 tsp	Worcestershire sauce
1/2 tsp	salt
1/8 tsp	pepper

Grated Parmesan cheese

Pre-heat oven to 450°F (230°C). Have ready 24 (2 inch) tiny tart pans. Roll pastry very thin, and cut into 24-3 inch rounds. Use these rounds to line the tart pan. Combine all ingredients except the Parmesan cheese. Spoon into pastry lined tart pans, about 2/3 full. Sprinkle each tart with 1/4 tsp Parmesan cheese. Bake 5 minutes at 450°F (230°C). Reduce temperature to 300°F (150°C) and continue baking 15 to 20 minutes longer or until filling is set. Cool slightly, then lift out of pan(s) and serve immediately. Makes 24 small quiches.

Cheese Dreams

1 package	cream cheese, (8 oz)
1 package	grated extra old cheese, (8 oz)
1 cup	butter

Melt all ingredients in top of double broiler. Let cool.

4	egg whites

Unsliced sandwich bread.

Beat egg whites until very stiff. Blend into cooled mixture of butter and cheese. Remove all crusts from sides of loaf. Cut bread into 1 inch cubes. With hands dunk cubes into cheese mixture until completely coated. Place on a cookie sheet lined with parchment paper. Freeze until firm. Place in a plastic bag until needed. Cook in a 400°F (200°C) oven for 10 minutes until lightly brown. Keep in freezer indefinitely. Serve piping hot.

Treble Cheese Dip

1 cup	cottage cheese
1 package	cream cheese with pimento, (4 oz)
1/3 cup	Gorgonzola cheese
2 tbsp	cognac
1	garlic clove, crushed

Salt to taste
Dash of Worcestershire sauce

In a blender, blend all ingredients together to make them smooth. Chill to blend flavours. Makes about 1 1/2 cups.

Bouchés

1/2 cup	butter
1 cup	water
1 cup	all-purpose flour
1/4 tsp	salt
4	eggs

In a saucepan, combine butter and water. Bring to a boil. Beat in flour and salt all at once. Continue cooking, beating vigorously until mixture leaves side of pan. Remove from heat and cool slightly.

Then add eggs, one at a time. After adding each egg, beat vigourously until smooth and glossy. Chill thoroughly. Drop batter from a spoon, 2 inches apart, onto greased baking sheet or one covered with parchment paper. Mound and swirl each top.

Bake in a pre-heated oven at 375°F (190°C) for 30 to 40 minutes. Cool. Slit sides, turn off oven and let dry in oven. Cool. Fill with filling of your choice. (For small bouchés, cook for 25 to 30 minutes.)

Seafood Stuffed Pitas

20 mini	whole wheat pitas
1/2 cup	cooked small shrimp, chopped
1/2 cup	crab meat, chopped
1 tbsp	fresh dill, chopped
1/4 cup	mayonnaise
1/4 tsp	garlic powder
Salt and Pepper	
Leaf lettuce	

Cut mini pitas in half. Combine shrimp and crab meat with dill, mayonnaise and seasonings. Stuff into each pita half. Makes 40.

Dilled Vegetable Toss

Any quantity of tomato wedges, cucumber or zucchini, celery and radishes. Slice or chop all the vegetables. Place in a covered bowl. Mix and add 1 cup yogurt, 3/4 tsp fresh dill and 1/2 tsp celery salt. Cover and let stand in refrigerator for 1 hour. Serve on a bed of shredded lettuce.

Mushroom, Lettuce Salad with Garlic Dressing

Garlic dressing:

1 cup	salad oil
1/3 cup	white wine vinegar
3	garlic cloves, finely minced
1 tsp	thyme leaves
1	bay leaf

Salad:

Lettuce for 8 servings

1 cup	fresh mushrooms, sliced
1/4 cup	capers, drained

Dressing Preparation:

Shake all ingredients in a jar. Store, covered, in the refrigerator. Remove bay leaf and shake well before serving. Makes 1 1/3 cups.

Salad preparation:

Combine ingredients. Toss with about 1 1/2 cup dressing. Serve extra dressing on the side.

Spinach and Bean Sprout Salad

1 cup	fresh bean sprouts
2/3 cup	raw spinach
2/3 cup	water chestnuts, sliced

Wash bean sprouts and drain thoroughly. Add spinach and water chestnuts to bean sprouts and toss well. Serve with oil and vinegar dressing or the garlic dressing recipe above.

Christmas Vegetable Trays

1	small cauliflower
1	bunch broccoli
1	English cucumber
2 cups	cherry tomatoes
1 lb	snow peas

Now Serving

204

Arrange the snow peas around the outside edge of the platter with a fan-like appearance. Platter should preferably be round. You may wish to use a large dinner plate. In a wreath like fashion, alternating white and green vegetables. Use the cherry tomatoes to add colour. Place a bowl of dip in the middle.

You can also use the cauliflower, broccoli and cherry tomatoes to make a Christmas tree using the tomatoes as ornaments for the tree. The cauliflower can be used to look like snow around the tree. Use the stalk of the broccoli for the trunk. Serve dip to one side.

Chicken Pecan Spread

1 lb.	boneless chicken breast
1 cup	chicken stock
1	bay leaf
1	small onion, thickly sliced
1 sprig	parsley
1/2 tsp	crumbled dried thyme
1 tsp	pepper
1/2 cup	mushrooms, chopped
1/4 cup	yogurt
1 tsp	salt
1/2 tsp	tarragon
1/2 cup	whipping cream
1/2 cup	pecans, chopped

Place chicken in a single layer in a skillet. Pour in stock to cover. Add bay leaf, onion, parsley, thyme and pepper. Bring to a boil. Reduce heat, cover and simmer for 10 minutes. Remove from heat, let cool.

Meanwhile, in a small bowl, combine yogurt and spices. Chop chicken coarsely. Add to above mixture. Stir in mushrooms and blend well. Whip cream until firm, fold into chicken mixture. Fold in all but 2 tbsp pecans. Transfer to serving bowl and garnish with pecans. Serve with vegetables or crackers.

Cracked Whole Wheat Bread

1 cup	lukewarm water
1 tsp	granulated sugar
2 tbsp	yeast
2 cups	lukewarm water
1/3 cup	vegetable oil
1/2 cup	brown sugar
1 tbsp	salt
6 cups	all-purpose flour
3 cups	whole wheat flour
1/2 cup	cracked wheat (bulgar)

Dissolve sugar in one cup of lukewarm water in a large warmed bowl. Sprinkle yeast over the water and sugar mixture. Let stand 10 minutes. Stir this solution until well blended, making sure yeast is dissolved.

Into this mixture, stir the remaining water, sugar, oil, and cracked wheat. Beat and then stir in flour one cup at a time. Mix until dough requires hand mixing. Keep mixing dough until dough is hanging together and moist.

Scrape dough out of bowl onto a well-floured surface. Sprinkle with flour and knead. Keep turning the dough as you knead and sprinkle with flour. Knead for several minutes until dough becomes smooth and elastic and does not stick to your hands.

Place dough in a lightly greased mixing bowl and cover with a dampened cloth. Place in a warm draft free location and let rise until doubled, about 2 hours. To test, stick two fingers into the centre of the dough. If the indentation remains, the dough is ready to make into loaves. Divide dough into three parts and shape into loaves. Place into greased bread pans and let rise an additional 1 hour until dough has risen above the top of the pan.

Bake in a 400°F (200°C) oven for 20 minutes. Remove from pan and cool on rack. Makes three loaves.

You are Cordially Invited

Mrs. No-Name reminds me of this story when I remind her about her mishaps in the kitchen. I was giving a dinner party for 10, serving roast pork with grapefruit sections. While the dinner was cooking, we enjoyed a few h'or d'oeuvres and cocktails. Just as I was about to call everyone to dinner, I happened to glance at the recipe. It read "Add the grapefruit juice and cook ANOTHER HOUR!" (I quietly had heart failure). Even if I offered everyone another drink, stretched out the first course, there would still be about 30 minutes to kill. I turned up the oven and made a confession to my guests. While we ate very late, it was well worth the wait and I learned a valuable lesson: read the recipe thoroughly.

I have also found that when preparing a meal for a large number of people, it is wise to make a timetable for all the separate dishes so that you can stay on schedule with ease.

I love cooking for company as it gives me a chance to experiment with different dishes which small children may not like. Entertaining at home has become more popular. I have included some recipes which will enable you to start cooking in advance so that you are not too tuckered out by the time your guests arrive. Good luck!

Brunch for Four

        Fruit platter
        Lobster Roll
        Orange Almond Coffee Cake
        White wine (Moreau Blanc)

Créme Fraiche

1 cup	whipping cream
1/2 cup	sour cream
Grated Peel of one lemon	
4 tsp	lemon juice
2 tsp	granulated sugar

In a small bowl, mix whipping cream and sour cream until smooth. Cover and let stand until thick, at room temperature, about 24 hours. Stir in lemon peel, juice and sugar. Cover and refrigerate. This will keep for at least 3 days. Makes about 1 1/2 cups.

Fruit Platter

Choose a variety of fresh fruits — melon, cantaloupe, strawberries, bananas, pineapple, grapes or pears. Arrange bite-sized pieces of fruit on a large platter. Serve creme fraiche in separate bowl. l spoon some on each serving of the fruit.

Lobster Roll

1/4 cup	unsalted butter
1/3 cup	all-purpose flour
1 1/2 cups	hot milk
6	eggs, separated
1 tsp	salt
1/4 tsp	freshly ground pepper
Dash cayenne pepper	
1/4 tsp	ground nutmeg
2 tbsp	freshly grated Parmesan cheese

Lobster Filling

1 can	lobster meat, (8 oz)
1 package	cream cheese, (8 oz)
2 tbsp	sour cream
1	red pepper, finely chopped
1	green pepper, finely chopped
1/4 cup	fresh dill, chopped
2 tbsp	fresh parsley, chopped
2 tbsp	chili sauce

Pinch basil
1 tbsp	brandy

Pinch garlic powder
Salt, pepper and lemon juice

Line a jelly roll pan with dampened parchment paper. Dust lightly with flour. In a heavy saucepan, melt butter and whisk in flour, cook without browning. Whisk in hot milk; cook, stirring constantly, until mixture comes to a boil and thickens. Remove from heat. Beat egg yolks, adding a few tablespoons of the hot sauce, then beat egg yolk mixture into sauce. (This is done to bring the egg yolks up to the same temperature as the cooked mixture to prevent the egg yolks from curdling.) Season to taste with salt, pepper, cayenne and nutmeg. Cool slightly.

Beat egg whites until stiff but not dry; gently fold into sauce. Spread mixture evenly in pan and bake at 375°F (190°C) for 20 to 25 minutes. Roll should be firm to the touch. Let cool 5 minutes. Sprinkle roll with Parmesan. Place clean tea towel over top and invert roll onto tea towel. Carefully remove paper. Trim edges.

Lobster Filling: In a blender, combine all ingredients. Taste and adjust seasonings. Spread filling evenly over roll. Be careful so as not to break the surface. Using the tea towel as a guide, form the roll into a tube-like appearance, starting at the narrow end. Roll lengthwise. Place on a long platter. To make the dish look even more attractive cut each end on a diagonal. Garnish with parsley sprigs and remaining filling. Serve chilled or at room temperature.

Orange Almond Coffee Cake

1/2 cup	sliced almonds
2 cups	all-purpose flour
4 tsp	baking powder
1/2 tsp	salt
2 tbsp	granulated sugar
1/2 cup	shortening
1	egg
1/2 cup	milk
2 tbsp	orange juice
2 tbsp	melted butter
1/4 cup	granulated sugar
1 tbsp	grated orange rind

Glaze:

1 cup	icing sugar
2 tbsp	orange juice
1 tbsp	grated orange rind

Pre-heat oven to 425°F (220°C). While preparing coffee cake, spread almonds in a cake pan, and toast lightly 3 to 4 minutes in the oven. Combine flour, baking powder, salt and 2 tbsp sugar. Finely cut in shortening or butter. Beat egg lightly with milk and orange juice. Add to dry ingredients all at once, stirring with a fork to make a soft slightly sticky dough. Turn out on lightly floured board and knead very lightly about 10 times. Roll out to a rectangle, 9 x 12 inches. Brush with melted butter. Sprinkle with a mixture of 1/4 cup sugar and 1 tbsp orange rind. Reserve 2 tbsp almonds for topping and sprinkle the rest over the dough. Roll up from the widest side. Cut into 12-1 inch slices with a sharp knife. Arrange rolls in a single layer in a greased 9 inch round cake pan.

Bake in 425°F (220°C) oven for 20 minutes or until golden brown and baked in the centre. Invert onto cake rack, let cool 10 minutes, then transfer to serving plate. Combine drizzle ingredients and drizzle over coffee cake. Serve warm. May be re-heated, wrapped in foil, in moderate oven, about 15 minutes. To serve, cut into wedges or separate rolls. Makes 8 to 12 servings.

Champagne Lunch for Two

Crab Melon Appetizer
Chicken à la Chemise
Baked Fudge Pudding
Henkle Trocken Champagne

Crab/Melon Appetizer

1 can ....crab meat
1 ....honeydew melon, sliced and peeled
Lettuce
Lemon
Parsley

Arrange chilled crab meat on two chilled plates. Slice melon in crescent shapes and place on plate. Squeeze small amount of lemon over crab meat. You may wish to put crab meat on a lettuce cup rather than directly on the plate. Garnish with sprig of parsley.

Chicken à la Chemise

1/2 cup	soft butter
1 package	cream cheese, (4 oz), at room temperature
1/4 tsp	salt
1 tbsp	all-purpose flour
4	medium-sized chicken breasts, skinned, boned and flattened
Salt and Pepper	
1/4 lb	cooked shrimp
1/2 cup	white wine
4 1/2 tbsp	butter
2	green onions, finely chopped
4	large mushrooms, finely chopped
1 1/2 tsp	all-purpose flour
1/4 tsp	salt
1/16 tsp	pepper
1 pinch	dried leaf of tarragon
1/4 cup	parsley, finely chopped
2 tbsp	butter
2 tsp	butter
1	egg yolk
1/4 cup	light cream

Cream 1/2 cup butter and cream cheese together. Add 1 tbsp of flour and 1/4 tsp salt. Mix with a fork until blended. Gather into a ball and wrap in parchment paper and chill.

Lay out chicken pieces, skinned side down. Sprinkle lightly with salt and pepper.

Chop shrimp into bite-sized pieces. Heat 3 tbsp of butter in a medium saucepan over high heat. Add onions and mushrooms and stir 3 minutes. Reduce heat to medium and sprinkle in 1 1/2 tsp flour, 1/4 tsp salt, pepper and tarragon. Stir to blend. Remove from heat and stir in wine. Return to heat and stir until boiling, thickened and smooth. Stir in parsley and remove from heat. Add 2 tbsp of mixture to shrimp, blending well.

Divide shrimp mixture evenly among chicken pieces (a heaping tablespoon each) placing it toward one end. Fold the other end over stuffing and press around edges to seal the meat to itself. Heat butter in large skillet over medium heat and add chicken pieces. Cook until lightly browned about 2 minutes per side and then cool.

Heat oven to 425°F (220°C). Have a large cookie sheet ready. Divide cream cheese pastry into 4 equal pieces. Roll each piece into a thin oval large enough to wrap around each piece of chicken to make a turnover. After wrapping each, crimp pastry edges to seal. Put on a cookie sheet.

Beat egg yolk and water with a fork and brush each turnover (not edges). Prick tops.

Bake until well-browned, 15 to 20 minutes. While turnovers are baking, heat the remainder of the onion-mushroom mixture and stir in cream. Serve chicken hot, topped with sauce.

Steam your selection of fresh vegetables. Snow peas and carrots add colour to the plate.

Baked Fudge Pudding

3/4 cup	margarine
3/4 cup	granulated sugar
1 1/2 cups	all-purpose flour
2 1/2 tsp	baking powder
1/2 tsp	salt
3/4 cup	milk
3/4 cup	chopped nuts

Topping:

1/4 cup	cocoa
3/4 cup	brown sugar
1/4 tsp	salt
1 cup	boiling water

Cream together the margarine and sugar until fluffy. Sift together the flour, baking powder and salt. Add to margarine mixture alternately with the milk. Stir in the nuts. Spoon batter into greased pudding dish or 9 x 9 inch cake pan. Combine cocoa, brown sugar and salt. Sprinkle cocoa mixture over pudding batter. Gently pour boiling water over top. Bake in a pre-heated 375°F (190°C) oven for about 25 minutes, or until toothpick inserted in middle comes out clean. Serve warm.

(Recipe courtesy of Recipes Only, October 1987, Page 254, Issue 24).

Summer Lunch for Two

Chilled Cucumber Soup
Seafood Pineapple Salad
Pumpernickel Bread
Fresh Lemon Mousse
Cuvée Speciale (White)

Chilled Cucumber Soup

1/2	cucumber
3/4 cup	plain yogurt
1/2 can	cream of celery soup

Coarsely chop the cucumber (no need to peel it) and place in a blender. Add remaining ingredients and process until smooth. Cover and place in the refrigerator until well chilled. Serve very cold with a slice of cucumber as garnish in chilled soup bowls.

Seafood Pineapple Salad

2 cans	crab meat, (5 oz), drained
1	ripe pineapple
1/2 cup	celery, thickly sliced
1/4 cup	green pepper, diced
1/4 cup	pecans, coarsely chopped
1/4 cup	plain yogurt
2 tbsp	chili sauce
1 tbsp	lemon juice
1	hard cooked egg, finely chopped

Set aside a few pieces of crab meat to garnish the salads. Slightly break up the remaining meat. Cut pineapple lengthwise, through leaves and bottom, into two halves. Loosen flesh of pineapple with paring knife and remove flesh, being careful not to break the shell of the pineapple.

Dice pineapple flesh and measure out one cup for the salad. (Use any left over pineapple in Sweet and Sour Pork recipe on page 196).

Combine crab, pineapple, celery, green onion and pecans in a bowl and toss together lightly. Combine the yogurt, chili sauce, lemon juice and egg and add to crab mixture, tossing lightly again. Pile crab mixture into hollowed out pineapple shells. Garnish with pieces of crab.

Pumpernickel Bread

3 packages	dry active yeast
1 1/2 cups	water
1/2 cup	dark molasses
2 tbsp.	caraway seed
1 tbsp.	salt
2 tbsp.	soft shortening
2 3/4 cups	rye flour
2 3/4 cups	all-purpose flour
1/4 cup	cornmeal

Soften dry active yeast in warm water. Combine molasses, caraway seed, salt, shortening, rye flour, about 1 cup of all-purpose flour and the softened yeast. Beat until smooth. Add enough of the remaining flour to make a stiff dough. Turn out onto lightly floured board and knead for about 10 minutes until elastic and smooth. Place dough in a greased bowl, turning once to grease surface. Cover and let rise in a warm place until doubled. (About 1 1/2 hours).

Punch down and divide into 2 parts. Cover and let rest 10 minutes. Round each part into a smooth ball. Place on opposite corners of a cornmeal covered baking sheet. Cover and let rise until double. (About 30 minutes). Bake loaves in a 375°F (190°C) oven for 30 to 35 minutes. Makes two round loaves.

Fresh Lime Mousse

1 package	unflavoured gelatin
1/4 cup	cold water
3/4 cup	granulated sugar
2/3 cup	lime juice
4	egg whites
Dash of salt	
1 cup	whipping cream, whipped

Mix the gelatin in the cold water to soften, about 5 minutes. Add 1/3 cup of sugar and set over boiling water to dissolve sugar. Stir in lime juice when dissolved and then chill until syrupy. Beat egg whites until foamy, and then add 1/4 cup of sugar. Beat into soft peaks. Fold into chilled gelatin mixture. Fold in the whipped cream.

Serve in parfait glasses and garnish with slices of lime. You may wish to add a touch of green food colouring to make the dessert more colourful.

Romantic Dinner for Two

Asparagus and Shrimp Salad
Chicken Abundance or Tino's Special
Wild Rice
Chocolate Dipped Strawberries and Kiwi Fruit
Lion Blanc (Dry White Wine)

Asparagus and Shrimp Salad

3/4 lb .... shrimp
1 .... thin slice of lemon
1 .... small slice of onion
Small piece of bay leaf
3 .... peppercorns
1 .... sprig celery leaves
1/2 tsp .... salt
Boiling water
1 can .... asparagus spears
1/3 cup .... olive oil
1/3 cup .... lemon juice
1/4 tsp .... dried tarragon
1/4 tsp .... dry mustard
1/2 tsp .... salt
1/4 tsp .... paprika
Lettuce

Combine shrimp in saucepan with lemon, onion, bay leaf, salt, peppercorns and celery leaves. Add boiling water to cover. Bring to a boil, turn down heat, cover and simmer about 5 minutes. Shrimp should be bright pink. Drain, shell if necessary, and clean shrimp. Cool and chill. (If you have a cat, it will go crazy while you cook the shrimp).

Put asparagus spears and shrimp in a single layer in a glass dish. Combine oil, lemon juice, tarragon, mustard, 1/2 tsp salt and paprika and pour over shrimp and asparagus. Cover and chill very well, spooning marinade over the food occasionally. Drain shrimp and asparagus at serving time. Cover 2 salad plates with lettuce. Divide up the food for each plate. Spoon a little of the marinade over the salad.

Chicken Abundance

2	green onions, chopped
1/4 cup	cream cheese
1 tbsp	butter
1 tbsp	sharp old cheese
2 tsp	vermouth
1/8 cup	grated Swiss cheese
Pinch nutmeg	
4	chicken breasts, boned and skinned
2 1/2 tsp	hot mustard
1 cup	all-purpose flour
1	egg
1 cup	milk
1 cup	bread crumbs
2 tbsp	oil
2 tbsp	clarified butter

Put green onions in a blender and process until finely chopped. Scrape down sides of glass and add the cream cheese. Process until smooth. Add the vermouth and the nutmeg and process until completely mixed. Place this mixture into the refrigerator until it is firm.

When firm, remove from bowl and divide into four cylindrical rolls. Roll each of these in the Swiss cheese. Place the chicken breasts between parchment paper and pound until they are flat and thin. Spread some of the hot mustard on each breast.

Place the cheese cylinders in the middle and roll the breasts around the cheese, making sure the cheese is completely covered. With a fork, whisk the egg and milk together. Roll the chicken breasts in the flour, then in the egg-milk mixture and then in the bread crumbs. Refrigerate until very cold. A half an hour before serving, sauté the breasts in the oil and butter until golden on all sides. Bake in a 350°F (180°C) oven for 20 to 25 minutes until chicken is firm to the touch.

Tino's Special

This dish is one of the best ways to serve filet mignon that I know. Cooked in butter over high heat, all the juices of the meat are sealed inside.

Filet mignon for four (about 1/2 lb each). Trim off all fat.

> 1/2 lb butter
> Salt
> Pepper (freshly ground black)
> Worcestershire sauce

Melt butter in a large pan over high heat until it begins to bubble and separate. Meanwhile, shape meat with backs of two large spoons until uniform in size. Sprinkle meat with salt and pepper.

Place meat in the pan of butter and cook (turning only once) until meat is cooked to your taste preference. This usually takes about 15 minutes for medium rare. Serve with a small selection of fresh vegetables. If desired, spoon some of the buttered sauce over the meat at serving time.

Chocolate Dipped Strawberries and Kiwi Fruit

> 1 cup .... unsalted butter
> 1/4 cup .... granulated sugar
> 4 .... egg yolks
> 2 tbsp .... Frangelico
> 2 tsp .... vanilla
> 1 cup .... semi-sweet chocolate, melted and cooled
> 1 cup .... whipping cream
> 1 quart .... strawberries

In a mixing bowl, cream together butter and sugar. Beat in egg yolks, vanilla and Frangelico. Blend in chocolate. Whip cream lightly and stir into chocolate mixture. Turn into 3 cup mould or small pots. Chill eight hours or longer. Serve with sliced kiwi fruit and strawberries along with vanilla wafer cookies.

Entertaining with Flair for Four

Vichyssoise
Mediterranean Fish and Seafood
Saffron Rice
Polish Cheesecake

Vichyssoise

1	medium onion, chopped
2 tsp	margarine
2	medium potatoes, chopped
1	small celery stock, sliced
1 can	chicken broth
1/4 tsp	salt
1 cup	half and half cream
1/4 tsp	pepper
1/2 cup	half and half cream
	Chives

Cook all the ingredients in a medium saucepan, except one half cup of the half and half cream for about 35 to 40 minutes. Vegetables should be tender.

Press through a sieve. Put back in the saucepan and add half and half. Heat over medium heat. Refrigerate and serve cold. Garnish with chives.

Mediterranean Fish and Seafood

1/4 cup	olive oil
1	garlic clove, minced
1	medium onion, finely chopped
1	bay leaf, crumbled
1/2 tsp	dried thyme
1 tsp	granulated sugar
1/4 cup	dry white wine
1 can	tomatoes, (28 fl. oz)
2 tbsp	parsley, chopped
1/2 tsp	salt
14 tsp	black pepper
1 lb	large, raw shrimp
1 1/2 lb	halibut steak, cut 1 inch thick

1/2 lb	feta cheese
1/2 cup	dry bread crumbs
1/4 cup	melted butter
1/4 cup	parsley, chopped

Heat oil in a medium saucepan and cook onion and garlic gently 3 minutes. Do not brown. Stir in bay leaf, thyme, sugar, wine, tomatoes, parsley, salt and pepper, bring to a boil. Reduce heat, cover and simmer 30 minutes. Sauce should be fairly thick — if it isn't, simmer uncovered for a few minutes more. Shell and de-vein shrimp. Skin and bone halibut and cut into 1 inch cubes. If you intend to bake the dish immediately, heat oven to 450°F (230°C).

Butter a large shallow baking dish, about 13 x 9 x 2 inches. Crumble feta cheese into the baking dish and spread it evenly. Combine bread crumbs, melted butter or margarine and parsley. Pour the tomato mixture over the cheese. Wrap each halibut cube in the curve of a shrimp and set in the tomato sauce in a single layer, pressing down so they are nearly covered. Continue until all are used, filling any spaces with leftover cubes of fish. Sprinkle with bread crumb mixture. Bake 20 minutes or just until fish is tender and dish is hot. Or refrigerate, covered, if you are baking it later.

(Recipe courtesy of Recipes Only, Nov/Dec.1983, Page 184, Issue 3).

Polish Cheesecake

1 1/2 cups	graham cracker crumbs
1/4 cup	melted butter
1/4 cup	granulated sugar

Combine crumbs, melted butter, sugar and line bottom and sides of a well-buttered 9 inch springform pan. Chill well.

6	egg whites, stiffly beaten
2 packages	cream cheese, (8 oz each)
1 cup	granulated sugar
1 tbsp	all-purpose flour
6	egg yolks, well beaten
2 tbsp	grated lemon rind
1 cup	sour cream
Cherry pie filling	
Cinnamon sticks	
Whipping cream	

Pre-heat oven to 350°F (180°C). Cream together cheese, sugar, flour and stir in egg yolks and lemon rind. Stir in sour cream. Gently fold in egg whites. Pour this mixture into the springform pan and bake at 350°F (180°C) for 1 hour. At the end of an hour, turn off the oven and open the door just a crack. Over the next hour, open the door slightly every now and then until the door is fully open. (This procedure keeps the cake from falling. It is very important to do this without the presence of children who are likely to be bouncing around). Refrigerate and serve with cherry pie filling spiced with cinnamon sticks. Just before serving, I heat the pie filling slightly with cinnamon sticks in a saucepan over medium heat and then pour the filling over the top of the cake. You can allow it to drip over the sides. The cake can be garnished with whipped cream.

Dinner for Four

Coquilles St. Bernard
Veal Romano
Noodles with Poppy Seeds
Crepes Frangelico
Côtes de Luberon (Dry French Red)

Coquilles St. Bernard

I have replaced scallops and Swiss cheese with shrimps and mozzarella, just for a change. This appetizer can be prepared the day before, kept in the refrigerator and popped into the oven for 12 minutes prior to serving at 350°F (180°C).

3 tbsp	butter
1 lb	shrimp
1/2 cup	mushrooms, sliced
1/4 cup	green onions, finely chopped
1	garlic clove, finely chopped
3 tbsp	butter
3 tbsp	all-purpose flour
1/2 tsp	salt
Pinch of pepper	
2 cups	milk
1/4 cup	Mozzarella cheese, finely grated
2 tbsp	dry white wine
1/4 cup	fine dry bread crumbs
1 tbsp	butter

Heat 3 tsp of butter in a frying pan until foamy. Add shrimp and cook until lightly browned. Add mushrooms, green onion and garlic. Cook until fish is tender. Meanwhile, in a saucepan, melt 3 tbsp of butter. Blend in mixture of flour, salt and pepper. Gradually stir in milk, cheese and white wine. Cook, stirring constantly, until thickened. Blend in shrimp mixture and fill 16 greased scallop shells. Sprinkle with dry bread crumbs. Dot with butter. Bake at 350°F (180°C) for 10 minutes.

Veal Romano

1/4 cup	all-purpose flour
1 tbsp	sweet paprika
1 tsp	garlic powder
1 tsp	salt
1/4 tsp	pepper
1	veal steak (about 2 1/2 lbs)
2 tbsp	olive oil
4	medium onions, thinly sliced
1 lb	mushrooms, sliced
2 tbsp	butter
1 cube	chicken bouillon
1/2 cup	boiling water
1/2 cup	white wine
2 tbsp	brandy
1 cup	sour cream
1/4 tsp	oregano

Cooked egg noodles for four (see following)

Combine flour, paprika, garlic powder, salt and pepper in a shallow dish. Cut veal steak into 4 serving pieces. Dip in flour mixture to coat both sides. Heat olive oil in an electric frying pan. Add onions and cook gently. Cook until tender crisp. Add mushrooms and sauté lightly. Push vegetables to one side and add butter to the pan. Add veal pieces and brown well on both side. Sprinkle with any remaining flour and stir to blend. Spoon onions and mushrooms over the meat. Reduce heat. Dissolve the chicken bouillon in the boiling water. Add white wine. Add mixture to skillet all at once. Stir to blend. Increase heat to medium high and bring to a boil. Reduce heat, cover and simmer for about one hour, until veal is tender. Spread noodles on a large platter. Top with pieces of veal. Stir sour cream, brandy and oregano into gravy in the pan. Pour over meat on top of the noodles.

Noodles with Poppy Seeds

3 tbsp	butter
6 oz	wide noodles, cooked
2 tsp	poppy seeds

Melt butter in a skillet. Add noodles and poppy seeds and stir together lightly until noodles are coated with butter.

Crepes Frangelico with Almond Cream Filling

Crepes:

1/3 cup	all-purpose flour, sifted
1 tbsp	granulated sugar
Dash salt	
1	egg
1	egg yolk
3/4 cup	milk
1 tbsp	butter, melted

Measure ingredients into a blender container or mixing bowl. Blend or beat with an electric beater until smooth. Refrigerate several hours or until thick. Heat a heavy 6-inch skillet until a drop of water will dance on the surface. Grease lightly and pour in 2 tbsp of batter. Lift skillet off the heat and tilt from side to side until batter covers the bottom evenly. Return skillet to heat and cook until underside of crepe is lightly browned (about 1 1/2 minutes). To remove, invert skillet over paper towels. Cook the remaining crepes the same way, just one side for about 1 1/2 minutes. Makes 10 crepes. Fill with Almond Cream Filling, recipe follows.

Almond Cream Filling

1 cup	granulated sugar
1/4 cup	all-purpose flour
1 cup	milk
2	eggs
2	egg yolks
3 tbsp	butter
2 tsp	Frangelico liqueur
1/2 tsp	almond extract
1/2 cup	ground almonds

Whipped Cream
Icing sugar
Grated unsweetened chocolate

Mix sugar and flour. Add milk; cook and stir until thick, then continue cooking and stirring 1 to 2 minutes longer. Beat the eggs and the egg yolks slightly; stir some of the hot mixture into the eggs to bring them up to the same temperature as the cooked mixture. Add the egg mixture to the hot mixture. While stirring, bring just to a boil and remove from heat. Stir in remaining ingredients, except whipped cream, icing sugar and grated chocolate. Cool to room temperature. Chill if not using right away.

To assemble:

Spread about 2 tbsp of the cream filling on the unbrowned side of each crepe. Roll up and place folded side down in a buttered 13 x 9 x 2 inch baking dish. Brush the crepes with melted butter and heat in a moderate oven for about 20 to 25 minutes. Sprinkle tops with grated unsweetened chocolate and sift icing sugar over all. Serve warm with whipped cream.

The Old Folk's Nightcap

I have a very good friend who recently entered the league of mature citizens. This person, possessed with a good, but at times perverse sense of humour, insisted I include this recipe. It is meant to be a tongue-in-cheek tribute to couples like my parents who have been married over 40 years and who are still very much in love. While they are beginning to advance in years, they are still very young at heart. I know they will chuckle when they read this. To my new mature citizen, you're looking great!

```
2 glasses .....................milk
2 ...............................digestive biscuits
2 ...............................mature citizens
1 ...............................small round table
2 ...............................chairs, soft
```

Pour milk into a small saucepan. Heat until lukewarm but not hot. Pour milk into two mugs with large handles. Place cookies on small plate. Set mugs of milk and cookies on a small round table. (Small enough for the two old folks to reach across easily). Seat the two lovebirds at the table. Dip the cookies into the milk prior to eating, to soften. Drink milk slowly. When finished, head straight to bed. Good night and sweet dreams!

Menus For Fine Dining At Home

It would be impossible to include all the recipes for every single dinner party I have given over the past 15 years. I thought perhaps my readers might be interested in at least having a menu guideline to help them plan their own soirées. Have fun mixing and matching the suggestions. All menus are as sure to please your guests as they have mine.

Appetizers:

Fresh Tomato Soup
Avocado Crab Cocktail
Watercress Salad
Caesar Salad
Vegetable Aspic Moulds
Escargots
Salad Panaché
Paté
Minted Melon Balls
Smoked Salmon with Rye Bread
Caviar
Crudites with Clam Dip
Stuffed Mushroom Caps
Chilled Asparagus Salad
Carrot Soup
Watercress Vichyssoise

Main Course:

Pasta Primavera
Sole with Almonds and Kiwi Fruit
Beef Curry/Saffron Rice
Cornish Hens with Cranberry Nut Stuffing
Pork Tenderloin Roast with Grapefruit Sections
Weiner Schnitzel
Roast Leg of Lamb
Pork Tenderloin Patties with Dijon Mustard
Fettucine with Diced Venison in Red Wine Sauce
Stir-fried Chicken with Pecans and Snow Peas
Tortellini with Pesto Sauce
Linguine alle Vongole (With Clam sauce)
Breast of Capon Stuffed with Lobster

Deserving Desserts:

Chocolate Soufflé
Strawberry Soufflé
Lime Mousse
Pots au Creme
Tarte au Citron
Double Chocolate Truffles
Rum Balls
Coffee Tortoni

Pears Vefour
Black Bottom Pie
Truffles
Chocolate Mousse
Biscuits Tortini

Our Daily Bread:

Pumpernickel
Swedish Light Rye
Dark Rye
Caraway Cheese Bread
Cornmeal Bread
Buttermilk Biscuits
Sesame Garlic Sticks
Raisin Bread

Other Tidbits

Metric Conversion Chart

Dry Measures:

1/4 tsp	1 ml
1/2 tsp	2 ml
1 tsp	5 ml
1 tbsp	15 ml
1/4 cup	50 ml
1/3 cup	75 ml
1/2 cup	125 ml
2/3 cup	150 ml
3/4 cup	175 ml
1 cup	250 ml

Mass:

1/4 lb	125 g
1/2 lb	250 g
1 lb	500 g
2 lb	1 kg

Temperature

Degrees F	Degrees C
300	150
325	160
350	180
375	190
400	200
425	220
450	230

Liquid Measures:

1/4 cup	50 ml
1/3 cup	75 ml
1/2 cup	125 ml
2/3 cup	175 ml
1 cup	250 ml

For a free copy of an 18-page brochure, Kitchen Metrics, write to Kitchen Metrics, Publication 1702, Information Services, Agriculture Canada, Ottawa, KlA 0C7.

Cookbooks:

With so many good Canadian cookbooks and magazines at our disposal it is hard to recommend them all. So I am going to defer to my favourites as many of them have stood me in good stead over the past 20 years. They are listed in alphabetical order so as not to put more emphasis on one than the other. I use them all regularly, all for different reasons.

Cookbooks:
Elegant Entertaining Cookbook - Myra Sable
Food That Really Schmecks - Edna Staebler
Menu Cookbook - Margo Oliver
More Food that Really Schmecks - Edna Staebler
The New Purity Cookbook
A Guide to Good Cooking - Five Roses Flour

Magazines:
    Canadian Living, monthly issues
    Chatelaine
    Food Magazine (Canadian Living)
    Recipes Only

Other honourable mentions, though not Canadian, are The Silver Palate, The Joy of Cooking, (this is a great reference book to have), Betty Crocker's Cooking for Two and McCalls' Superb Desserts.

Learning to cut up your own meat is perhaps one of the most important skills you can acquire, which in turn will save you money in the years to come. David Brown, of Meat Consultants International Inc. writes a weekly column for the Toronto Star instructing his readers on the ways and means of becoming your own butcher.

Look for a book by David, due out in 1989, or write to him with any questions about cutting up your own meat at P.O. Box 292, Station G, Toronto, Ontario, M4M 3G7.

Finally...

If we accept the premise that we must eat, it follows that someone must cook. If you are the designated chef, willingly or unwillingly, you can have fun in the kitchen. There is nothing more satisfying to the person who has prepared a meal or a special dessert than to see empty plates.

I remember my older sister Randy who, as a teenager, (a few years ago), made a Banana Sundae Cake. Randy and a friend spent about a total of 5 hours making this wonderful creation. I think it disappeared in less than 20 minutes, long before she had time to clean up the kitchen. Randy was furious, for they had spent so many hours creating this masterpiece. She learned that the disappearance of the cake was, in fact, a compliment to her skills in the kitchen.

While we all have successes and I hope you have many, we all experience a few disasters once in awhile. It can be upsetting to throw food away, especially if you have spent a great deal of time and money on the dish. In the event of such a situation, forge ahead. There is always another success waiting to be created. Learn to be creative and innovative.

This "epistle according to Mum" has come to an end (at last, you say)! It is usually at this stage of writing the book that I vow I shall never write another. Many months after it is published I am sure to say — "it was a piece of cake" (please pardon the pun). My reward for the many hours spent on this project will be if you enjoy the recipes and find some useful information to help you become a smart shopper and a good cook.

 If you find any errors in the text or the recipes, please write to me at:

Protter Publishing Corporation
357 Bay Street
Suite 701
Toronto, Ontario
M5H 2T7

They will be corrected in the next printing. Thank you.

Recipe Index